T0344159

INDEX ON CENSORSHIP
Volume 40 Number 1 2011
INDEX ON CENSORSHIP
Volume 40 Number 2 2011
Privacy!
IS DEAD!
pen

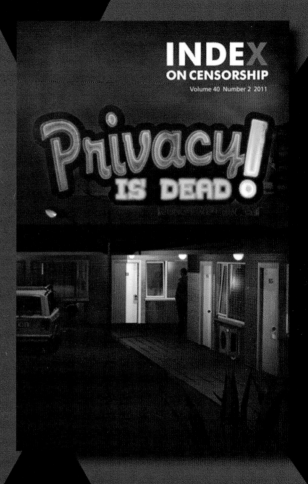

Index on Censorship

Free Word Centre, 60 Farringdon Road, London, ECIR 3GA

Volume 40 No 2 2011

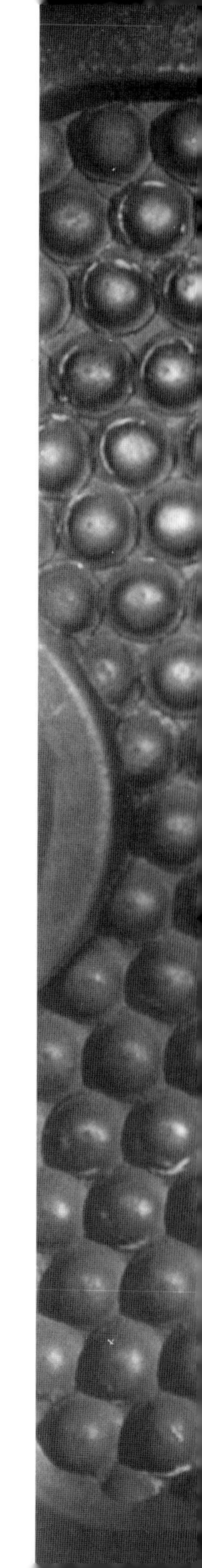

FRIEND OR FOE

Jo Glanville

Is privacy the friend or foe of free speech? Celebrities' use of injunctions and superinjunctions to stop the publication of stories about their private lives in the UK, and the perception that judges are inclined to weigh privacy in the balance at the expense of press freedom, continue to be a leading media story. In May, the former Formula One boss Max Mosley lost his attempt to create a European-wide law that would have made it mandatory for editors to give prior notification to the subjects of privacy stories, while Prime Minister David Cameron has voiced his concerns about judges' so-called creation of a privacy law. Read Joshua Rozenberg's interview with Mr Justice Eady for a rare response from a judge whose name has become most identified with privacy in the press [pp. 47–55].

The irony is that just as the right to privacy began to be viewed as a threat to media freedom, with the introduction of the Human Rights Act in 1998, it also became a necessity for free speech online. It is now one of the central issues of the digital communications age. Gus Hosein and Eric King, two leading campaigners, describe how the battle for privacy was lost in the 1990s, when governments and business were left to define the terms. The consequence is what we're living with now: data breaches and data loss because of systems that were not built with protection of privacy as a fundamental concern. 'If the US State Department can't be bothered to adequately secure its own network of inter-embassy communications, what chance is there that Facebook and Google will take better care of your personal messaging and commonly used search terms?'

What's the answer? Hosein and King think it's time for a policy debate. Icelandic MP Birgitta Jónsdóttir, who experienced the insecurity of the modern age at first hand, when the US Department of Justice requested her private information from Twitter last year in the fallout from WikiLeaks, would like to see the same human rights applied online as offline: '… these two worlds have fused and it is no longer possible to define them as distinct any more'

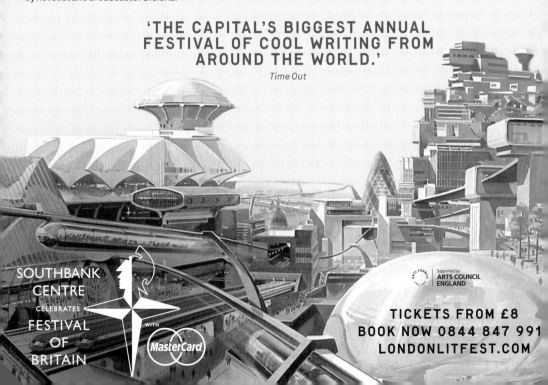

[pp. 102–106]. However, as Peter Fleischer, Google's chief privacy counsel, illustrates in an interview with Index, privacy legislation can also lead to some unworkable, and at times absurd, expectations online. Take the case of a German law that protects former criminals by shielding their identity in the media. In the online world, it's an almost impossible law to enforce. Even if all German websites obeyed the law, what about sites overseas that link to news stories mentioning former criminals: how would they be policed? Google believes that there need to be global privacy standards, and for harmonised data protection law. But coming up with laws that will protect citizens' rights while being practical for the digital age is one of the biggest challenges of our time.

Also in this issue of Index on Censorship you can read an exclusive interview with leading Egyptian journalist Ibrahim Eissa, winner of this year's Index on Censorship *Guardian* journalism award, a short story by Libyan writer Ibrahim al Koni, and Anthony Lester on blasphemy. Keep up with censorship news at www.indexoncensorship.org ❐

40(2): 1/5
DOI: 10.1177/0306422011413009
www.indexoncensorship.org

CONTENTS

2
3
6
7
10
14
15

Security camera
Credit: Brownstock/Alamy

DISPATCHES

After the revolution: Ibrahim Eissa on press freedom in Egypt

Generación Y: Yoani Sánchez on blogging in Cuba

A man waves an Egyptian flag in Tahrir Square hours before President Hosni Mubarak steps down from office on 11 February 2011
Credit: James May/Alamy

MUBARAK'S NEMESIS

Egypt's leading independent editor, **Ibrahim Eissa**, talks to Index about freedom of the press, revolution and the fight for democracy

In March, Ibrahim Eissa was honoured at Index on Censorship's Freedom of Expression Awards, winning the *Guardian* Journalism prize. One of the judges, Lindsey Hilsum, the international editor for Channel 4 News, who has reported on the revolution in Egypt, said she had been struck by how Eissa, along with the others on the shortlist, 'don't give up, whatever the forces brought to bear against them'.

Eissa has become a one-man barometer of Egypt's struggle for political and civic freedom. When the portly, friendly 45-year-old is running free and holding court on the nation's front pages and television screens, it means that things are opening up. But when Eissa is hounded from the scene and forced to operate from the margins, it heralds dark days.

That's exactly what happened last October when, in a swift series of events, Eissa's popular satellite talk show was taken off air and he was removed from his job as editor of the independent newspaper *al Dustour*. A talented writer with a savage wit, his trademark front-page columns gleefully targeted sacred cows. So his fall was no surprise.

His sacking came in the midst of a wider media crackdown in the run-up to Egypt's parliamentary elections in November, when President Hosni Mubarak's ruling National Democratic Party emerged victorious amid accusations of unprecedented vote rigging. Eissa even predicted his own professional demise in a front-page column a week before he lost his job, warning that the government would move to suppress the country's independent media voices. When the axe fell, he told the press: 'The regime is making a clear statement, instead of preventing vote rigging they banned speaking out against it … I feel sorry for the Egyptian press and media.'

This brought to ten the number of newspapers Eissa has worked on during his long career, most of which were closed down by the Mubarak regime. But he has also had to live with the threat of imprisonment. In 2006, he was sentenced to a year in prison for writing about a lawsuit personally accusing Mubarak of corruption. But by now the country's political dynamics had started to change, thanks in part to the emergence of the feisty, grassroots, opposition Kefaya movement, which directly challenged the taboo of criticising the president and his family. His sentence was reduced to a fine. In 2007, he received another sentence, this time of two months in jail, for crossing a major red line by writing that Mubarak's health was deteriorating. The following year the sentence was commuted by presidential decree. That same year, Eissa also received the Gebran Tueni Award, an annual prize of the World Association of Newspapers that honours an editor or publisher in the Arab region.

Since the revolution, Eissa has started an independent satellite TV channel and a newspaper, and his mission to promote a free, democratic Egypt is stronger than ever. On accepting his Index award in London he said: 'I came to you tonight from a country where the free journalist had no option but to lose his job, his freedom, his life, or maybe his mind, should he decide to oppose the ruler. I came to you from a country where a journalist worried about his "pen" more than what is written by this pen; where a journalist spends more time in interrogation and court rooms than in the office. But I also came from a country where words created a revolution, and where ink ran into rivers of people … I will stand in Tahrir Square, in the very same place where Egyptians died for freedom, and I will tell them: "I dedicate this Index award to you."' *Ashraf Khalil and Caroline Palmer*

Index: Since the overthrow of Hosni Mubarak, has there been a change in the way that the press covers politics? Is there more freedom of speech?

Ibrahim Eissa: Absolutely. There are three types of media in Egypt. The state media, which is directly owned by the state – in theory, it is owned by the people but in reality it is the state that owns it. Then there is the private media, which is owned by the private sector, that is by businessmen who are linked to the state, either as members of the National Democratic Party or by the fact that their business interests and economic situation depend on the state – which can declare them bankrupt, or punish them economically in other ways, at any time. There are also the newspapers owned by the political parties. All three types of media have been influenced by the revolution and have been changed as a result of it, but in different ways. The state media has reacted as though this revolution was a government. It has begun to suck up to the revolution and lend it its support just like it used to lend its support to the government. It has replaced Hosni Mubarak with the armed forces, so now it's 'the wisdom of the armed forces' and so on. So, the strategy is the same, hence the fear that the revolution might not have freed state media but just changed its allegiance.

Now with regard to the private media, it is in fact controlled by its own interests. On the one hand, it must show its support for the revolution, which everyone has an obligation to do, but on the other hand it must defend its own interests. So you find that private media is focusing on promoting stability, saying how the country needs it and so on. In other words, you will notice that all the signs of the counter-revolution are more present in the private media than in the state media. As for the party-owned media, it was never influential even prior to the revolution because it is the expression of weak parties which have no real support among the people and do not enjoy a wide distribution.

Index: So constraints remain, whether it's out of fear or self-interest?

Ibrahim Eissa: Yes. These constraints are imposed by the owners [of the media]. The constraints directly imposed by the state have been replaced by other constraints imposed by the journalist himself, or by the editors who are not sure what to do and are waiting for instructions. Notice that none of the leaders of the state press has changed. It is the same singer singing a different song, so it is no surprise that he should not have enough faith in the new song and that he should not be sufficiently loyal to it or willing to practise it. As for the private media, the constraints are imposed by the owners; that is, by their business interests. This is what we find on the media scene today.

Index: In your own case, you're obviously somebody who has always challenged the taboos. Are you now going further? Have your targets changed?

Ibrahim Eissa: The thing is that a free man never waits for the regime to change [to speak his mind], for he is a free man, and he is not a free man because there are instructions ordering him to be so. I think that, for me, the task at the moment is to safeguard the 'ceiling of freedom', to make sure it remains high in the face of everything, whether the current regime or the one yet to come. [To stand firm] in the face of the potential lowering of the ceiling, or a possible giving way by the media or the journalists. This is a very important side of the issue. The other side is that, just like you used to face up to state tyranny, you must now face up to the tyranny of the street; you must face up to the religious thought and the religious believers who want to impose their own view on Egyptian life and on the Egyptian public. You must be free of all the ideas that suck up to the street and support it even when it is wrong, because not everything the street might say is necessarily democratic and must be followed. The last point is the importance of developing the profession itself, developing ways to express your freedom, with the highest possible degree of artistry.

Index: When you consider that Egypt has been under dictatorship for decades, how do you go about helping journalists and the population out of the box that is censorship? Are there lessons to be learned from looking at what happened in 1989 after the fall of communism?

Ibrahim Eissa: I think that practising democracy and freedom is what will help people to understand freedom better, to explore it and believe in it. I do not think that what is needed is awareness lessons to enable the Arab mind in general, or the Egyptian mind in particular, to be free and walk away from censorship. What is needed is for one to lead the way, to set an example by walking away from censorship and speaking freely, writing freely and producing art freely. In this way, you can bring about an understanding of freedom among the people and force them to deal with it as a matter of course and a 'destiny' which it is not possible to give up again. However, we face two problems. Firstly, there is an old mentality, which has been shaped by years of repression and tyranny. Alongside this, or on top of this, there is a mentality that has been fostered by religious trends that revolve around conservatism, traditionalism, prohibition, the issuing of fatwas against any free idea that could emerge from art or writing or poetry. This is a real battle and a long one, by the way, and the last thing we need is to lose hope.

Protesters call for the prosecution o[illegible]ponsible for civilian deaths during January's revolution, Tahrir [illegible] Cairo, 8 April 2011
Credit: Barry Iverson/Alamy

Index: What practical steps are needed to increase the freedom of the press, considering that distribution and printing are owned by the state and that there are laws that restrict freedom of speech?

Ibrahim Eissa: Three steps are needed. The first step is to help with the establishment of free and independent newspapers and media, either by journalists starting their own newspapers or by presenters, producers and others starting their own satellite TV channels. The second step would be to put pressure from within and without, at the international and legal levels, against the legislation which, in its current form, prohibits the free ownership of newspapers and satellite channels and makes them subject to very tight restraints. The third step is to train journalists and instil in them the concepts of a free press, and to rehabilitate the rest who, in 30 years under the rule of Mubarak, only got to know one style of journalism and one form of freedom.

Index: It's a big job.

Ibrahim Eissa: [He laughs.] Very much so.

Index: In terms of your own career, when you were sacked from *al Dustour*, you set up a website. That's still going. Do you have any other plans?

Ibrahim Eissa: I have actually started a satellite TV channel with a number of my colleagues. The channel is called al Tahrir and has begun regular broadcasting, showing documentaries and video clips about the revolution, songs and recorded videos. Some of the stars of Egyptian media are with us, including Mahmoud Saad. This is the first satellite TV channel to be owned by journalists and media figures, which is important because I believe that this could set an example for other channels to follow. At the same time, I have started a newspaper, also called *al Tahrir,* with a number of public figures who own a company that issues *al Shuruq* newspaper. And also with us will be the same group who works on the website of al Dustour al Asli, which will retain its strong presence. In this way I will have done my duty: started a TV channel where I present a programme, started a newspaper where I will be the editor, and I have a website that runs for the people second by second and minute by minute.

Index: The last question: what hopes do you have that Egypt really will have a properly democratic government? Do you fear that one authoritarian power structure might be replaced by another?

Ibrahim Eissa at the 2011 Index on Censorship Freedom of Expression Awards in London, where he was presented with the Guardian *Journalism Award*
Credit: Karim Merie

Ibrahim Eissa: No. I think there is no way that the people who put an end to the rule of Mubarak and stood in the face of his dictatorship will once again allow the production of a dictator. I am anxious but I am not tense or scared, and I believe that through a civil struggle, a free media and new political parties, it is hard to imagine Egypt going back to the age of dictatorship. This does not necessarily mean the freedom which we long for and would like to see or dream of seeing in Egypt, but while we may not be London, we are certainly not going back to the former Cairo.

Ibrahim Eissa was talking to Jo Glanville. Translated by Nada Elzeer.

40(2): 14/22
DOI: 10.1177/0306422011409295
www.indexoncensorship.org

Yoani Sánchez working at her home in Havana, 9 February 20[illegible]
Credit: Desmond Boylan/Reuters

LIVING THE LIFE

Celebrated Cuban blogger **Yoani Sánchez** talks to Nick Caistor and Amanda Hopkinson

The Cuban authorities recently accused Yoani Sánchez and her 'Generación Y' blog of being part of a concerted 'cyberwar' against the government, now led by Raúl Castro. Yoani's blog is often blocked so that no one inside Cuba can read her work, but in the United States, Spain and the rest of Europe, many thousands follow her accounts of daily life. Yoani Sánchez does not write on overtly political topics, but her descriptions of the hassles and absurdities of life on the Caribbean island today paint an accurate picture that often clashes with the official version. According to *Time* magazine, she was one of the world's '100 most influential people' in 2008, together with Barack Obama, the Dalai Lama and Rupert Murdoch, but she insists she is simply a citizen who wishes to exercise the rights all Cubans should be free to enjoy.

Yoani lives with her husband, son and a large, friendly black-and-white dog. They occupy a 19th-floor apartment of a drab, weather-stained 1960s Soviet-style tower block behind several ministry buildings in the west of Havana. However, it is almost luxurious by the standards of the capital: it is relatively large and airy, boasts two bedrooms, and its tiny internal courtyard is crammed with tropical greenery. The living-room walls are lined with books. Many of the volumes are brought into the country by individuals, to be loaned out as part of the increasingly prevalent system of 'private libraries', a means of breaking the state's monopoly on publishing and distribution.

Yoani is now 35 years old, and her parents were part of the generation of the 1960s, raised in the first decade following 'the Triumph of the Revolution'. They shared the faith that Che Guevara's 'New Man' would combine with the state communism adopted by Fidel Castro and his regime to create a better world. Yoani recalls how they laboured long hours for scant pay, over and beyond their jobs. 'They sacrificed their lives to build a socialist heaven for their children,' she recalls.

By the time the Russians pulled out in the 1990s and the islanders were facing up to the stringencies of what Fidel Castro termed 'a special period in times of peace' – one that translated into further shortages, along with still less freedom of speech and movement – Yoani's parents finally lost faith in this promised paradise. 'They changed overnight. My father stopped being a Communist Party militant. My mother was no longer a leader in the communist youth movement. They became completely disillusioned, and that was the world I grew up in.'

This atmosphere led Yoani to look abroad for opportunities. Unlike many, however, she did not aim for Miami and life as a Cuban exile. Instead, she taught in Europe, spending two years in Switzerland, where she studied computer science and realised how powerful the new technologies could be.

On her return to Cuba in 2004, she put her mastery of the medium to practical use. She opened a web portal and with others began publishing online blogs. Since only 5 per cent of Cubans, almost exclusively officially sanctioned state employees, are currently allowed direct internet access, Yoani started using the large tourist hotels where business centres are intended for the use of resident foreign tourists.

Cuba has no internet cafes and the libraries do not offer online access. A small number of 'dissident' Cuban writers rely on weekly access of a few hours a week, granted via foreign embassies. Yoani is determined that if she is not permitted access to the internet in her living-room, she should at least be able to be free to walk into the only public centres available. She regards it as her right, as a Cuban: 'I prefer visiting hotels and confronting the system rather than just bypassing it by using the embassies. Anyone who does this automatically enters the system via servers in the countries of origin, rather than over a Cuban server.' When she was denied access on one occasion, she filmed the event on her phone and posted it online, immediately attracting 50,000 hits.

It was after Yoani took the decision in 2007 to put her name to her blogs that trouble with the regime began. As often happens with 'dissidents' in Cuba, she has been accused of being a CIA agent, and more recently of being part of a foreign-instigated 'cyberwar' against the regime. This has had predictable repercussions on her personal life: 'I don't consider myself paranoid, but people have been encouraged to ostracise me,' she says with a shrug. She says she can live with the constant surveillance of the building where she lives, but is worried about what might happen to her son. A star school pupil, he could be subjected to exclusion from tertiary education on spurious (non-academic) grounds. This would be another example of the way in which parents are punished through their children, by the unexplained refusal of university admission.

Occasionally the harassment has been more brutally direct. Yoani was physically assaulted in November 2009 and February 2010, when she was going to a meeting of the 'damas de blanco' – the women in white – who protested silently each week about the notorious detention of 75 journalists, writers and human rights activists arrested during the 'Black Spring' of 2003. She paused to show us how she was held down on the floor of a taxi with her knee pressed against her sternum, causing maximum pain with least visible effect. She also showed us how this has left her unable to turn her head from side to side, the apparent consequence of pressure on her cervical vertebrae. 'They prefer methods that cause lasting pain but don't

Generación Y

Timid coloured awnings are springing out of nowhere, big umbrellas are starting to sprout, with beneath them fruit smoothies, pork scratchings; some doorways are turned into improvised cafes with appealing offers. In recent days, all this and more has been growing on the streets of my city as a result of the new relaxation of restrictions on self-employment. Some of my neighbours are planning to start shoe-repair shops, or a place where they can repair fridges, while avenues and squares are being completely transformed as private initiative blossoms. The straitjacket imposed on initiative appears to have been loosened. Yet there are those who are still hanging back until they can be sure that this time the reforms to the Cuban economy are for real, and will not be revoked as they were in the 90s.

In the past few months, since it was announced that the number of permits for independent labour was to be increased, the results have been encouraging. We have begun to rediscover lost flavours, longed-for recipes, hidden comforts. More than 70,000 Cubans have taken out new permits to work for themselves, and thousands more are seriously considering the benefits of opening a small family business. Despite many people still being wary, despite the still excessive taxes and the lack of any wholesale market, these brand-new traders have begun to make an impact in a society characterised by its immobility. They can be seen installing their little stands, putting up brightly coloured signs advertising their wares, re-organising their homes to create cafes or to offer hairdressing or manicure services. Most of them are convinced that this time they are here to stay, because the system that in the past stifled and demonised them is no longer able to compete with them.

From the blog 'The rebirth of flavours'

produce an immediate show of blood.' She pointed out how counterproductive these violent acts of aggression can be: 'They had the opposite effect to that intended – there was a surge in support for us, and the attacks only made me more determined.'

Apart from instances of intimidation, the main restriction Yoani currently faces is that of not being able to travel abroad. In 2009, she was refused permission to leave the country in order to collect the prestigious Moors Cabot award for freedom of speech from Columbia University in New York. More recently, she has been denied a visa to travel to collect prizes in Germany and Spain for her work. 'They took my passport, and instead of giving me a visa, simply failed to return it. They do not need to refuse to [grant me a visa], they just do not give [my passport] back. So I cannot leave to go anywhere outside the island,' she adds.

Beyond what affects her personally, what most incenses Yoani is the amount of doublespeak and hypocrisy that the Cuban authorities indulge in. Showing us her ration card, she remarks that, for example, each Cuban is allocated six kilos of sugar per month. This is not because it grows in such abundance on the island (Cuba in fact now has to import from Brazil what for so long used to be its main crop) but because of the quantity of calories it contains. In this way the country avoids appearing poverty-stricken in terms of global statistics. Above all, the revolution would face ultimate shame and failure if Cuba were shown as a country where malnutrition affected the population.

Yoani relates the surge in street crime to the current economic crisis. 'Take the crime wave there has been here,' she continues. 'It hardly receives a mention, even in the [state-owned] media. The government's attitude is: if you don't talk about something, then it doesn't exist. The commonest crimes, like robberies and muggings, are rarely recorded. The police are complicit in this, for fear it could reflect badly on them; all state employees are constantly looking over their shoulder. We even hear, for example, about hospitals equipped with the latest technology, but not that they are lacking such basic materials as sheets or thermometers.'

Yoani is well aware that such criticisms are bound to make life harder for her in Cuba. But she insists that she is doing nothing wrong or 'unpatriotic' and that visibility and being completely open about what she is doing are her best defence. 'A blog is a way of talking to yourself. At the same time, you have to be completely transparent and honest with yourself to be able to explain to anyone who was not born in Cuba what this society is like.'

There are now at least a hundred 'alternative bloggers' in Cuba, despite the lack of official access to the internet. It is estimated that her own 'Generación Y' blogs are translated into 21 languages, but she has also moved on to the next stage. 'I'm really proud that I can reach 102,000 people on Twitter, whereas Fidel only has 93,000 followers. That's because his tweet is really boring.' Bringing an apparently new word into the Cuban vocabulary, she adds: 'But Raúl *no es twittero.*'

She is confident that the Castro regime cannot keep the lid on the free circulation of information on the island: 'The information monopoly is being broken thanks to satellite phones, the internet, all the new technological developments. More people are becoming aware of them every day, it's something you can't prevent.'

Yoani herself helps promote this spread of the use of new technologies by running courses on using the internet and Twitter, and on how to create new blogs and websites. She insists again that she has every right to do so, and that this is in no sense a 'war' on the Cuban government. The library she runs from home is to loosen the state's stranglehold on the publishing and circulation of books. 'I know many people have sent me hundreds of them, but not one has ever arrived,' she tells us.

Like many dissidents – the last of the Black Spring 75 has only just gone into involuntary exile – she is fiercely Cuban, and prefers to be able to live in her home country. Despite the risks to which she is now exposed, she insists she has no regrets: 'I am living the life I have chosen to live.'

We all need to leave the apartment at the same time, to go our separate ways. We agree to split up as we depart, in order to avoid attracting the attention of anyone who might be watching outside. However, this is Cuba and we have to wait ten minutes for the lift to arrive. We end up sharing it for the long drop down to street level. We emerge at the same time, studiously avoiding each other, and without bidding goodbye. Yoani puts on her sunglasses before we go out into the sunlight. ❐

40(2): 24/29
DOI: 10.1177/0306422011409982
www.indexoncensorship.org

Amanda Hopkinson is visiting professor of literary translation at both Manchester University and City University, London. She has published many books on Latin American culture and translated more from the Spanish, Portuguese and French

Nick Caistor is a freelance writer. He teaches journalism at UAE. Reaktion Books will publish his book *Fidel Castro: a critical life* next year

PRIVACY IS DEAD

LONG LIVE PRIVACY!

Credit: Brett Biedscheid

CODE BREAKERS

Journalists are being tarnished by the activities of professional privacy invaders. It is time they were renamed and shamed, argues **Brian Cathcart**

There is a confusion at the heart of British debates about privacy. We tend to speak of journalists, of their role, their rights, their responsibilities and very often their lack of restraint and how it should be addressed. But this is misleading, and prevents us from seeing some of the complexities and possibilities, because the word 'journalist', in this context, covers two very different groups of people. One group is the actual journalists, as traditionally understood, and the other is those people whose principal professional activity is invading other people's privacy for the purpose of publication.

The difference between the two, when you pause to consider it, is profound. Journalism is demonstrably valuable to society. It tells us what is new, important and interesting in public life, it holds authority to account, it promotes informed debate, it entertains and enlightens. For sure, it comes with complications. It is rushed and imperfect, it sometimes upsets people and in pursuit of its objectives it occasionally does unpleasant or even illegal things. But by and large we accept these less welcome aspects of journalism as part of the package, and we do so because journalism as a whole is in the

Glenn Mulcaire arrives at the Old Bailey, London, 26 January 2007
Credit: Rukhsana Hamid/Bloomberg

public interest. It does good, or to put it another way, we would be much poorer without it.

Invading people's privacy for the purpose of publication does not do good, though it may make money. In that industry, deception and payment for information are routine, not exceptional. The subject matter is almost never important – except to the victims, whose lives may be permanently blighted – and while a story may entertain, it does so only in the way that bear-baiting and public executions used to entertain. The whole activity exists on the border of legality, skipping from one side of the line to the other at its own convenience and without sincere regard for the public interest.

If they are so different, why do we tend to lump them together? A number of reasons. One is that journalists themselves are slow to draw the distinction because theirs is traditionally an open industry, without barriers and categories, and also because they don't tend to think of what they do in terms of doing good and being valuable. But there is also a more tangible explanation, which is that the privacy invaders do everything they can to blur the line. It is in their interest to be considered journalists, after all. They can shelter under the same umbrella and enjoy the same privileges as journalists. They can talk about freedom of expression, freedom of the press and serving the public interest; they can appeal to tradition and history and they can sound warnings about current and future censorship. This helps them to protect what they do.

Today, in 2011, the activities of the privacy invaders have provoked a crisis which threatens to compromise and damage the journalism that is done in the public interest. After a succession of scandals, the worst of them associated with Rupert Murdoch's *News of the World*, the demand for tighter legal constraints on the news media has reached a level not seen for many years. This is probably not another 'last chance saloon' episode, with empty warnings and hollow condemnations, as was seen in the early 1990s, because the centre of gravity in the debate has shifted. Many people in Parliament, the law and the media itself who were previously vital to the defence of press freedom are in despair. They watch in particular the phone hacking scandal, in which the *News of the World* has been forced to admit illegally accessing people's voicemails on an astonishing scale, and they feel that the press is out of control and unwilling to take responsibility for its failures. There is a strong chance that the next year or so will bring important change.

The greater the threat of effective press regulation, the more the privacy invaders can be counted upon to press their claim to be journalists, and so part of the free-speech tradition. They are like drowning men in the water, clinging on for dear life to those who have lifejackets. But journalists, for their part, may be approaching a moment of choice. Do they acknowledge the difference, the better to protect their own interests, or do they risk being dragged down into the depths by the sinking privacy invaders?

And it is not just a moment of choice for journalists. The reading public also needs a clearer understanding. We need to recognise privacy invasion for what it is, to accept that a luridly packaged, sensational, self-promoting and at the same time self-righteous product is actually bad for our collective health. And we need to grasp better the distinction between that and what is genuinely done in the public interest.

The most vivid recent example of the privacy invaders at work, and the one which most clearly shows that what they do is not journalism, is the case of Max Mosley, the former president of the Federation Internationale de l'Automobile. Because Mosley sued, details of a *modus operandi* which normally remains hidden were exposed. The story is well known, but details are worth revisiting.

In March 2008, the *News of the World* persuaded a woman who participated in private S&M parties with Mosley to film one of these events secretly, promising her £25,000 if the resulting story made the front page. A reporter was recorded showing her how to use the camera and saying how far away from Mosley she should stand 'when you want to get him to do the Sieg Heil'. The party took place and the paper got its film. There was no Sieg Heil, but some German was spoken in one role-play scene (by a participant who was German) and joke-shop prison uniforms were worn in another. In the paper's view, this established a useful connection – Mosley's father had led the wartime British fascist movement. The story appeared under the headline: 'F1 boss has sick Nazi orgy with 5 hookers'.

The next week, for a follow-up story, the paper approached two other women participants and told them to choose between being identified in print and giving an interview. They refused to cooperate, so the paper returned to the first woman. Her payment had been unilaterally reduced from the promised £25,000 to £12,000, but she was now told she could earn a further £8,000 if she gave an interview. (It was alleged in court that she too was threatened with exposure.) She agreed, but the court heard that her role in the interview involved nothing more than signing the first page of a text that had already been written, and which was altered between signature and publication. It appeared under the headline: 'Mosley hooker tells all'.

Sienna Miller has received £100,000 compensation from the News of the World *for hacking the actress's phone*
Credit: Ian West/PA

Besides the fact that it appeared in a newspaper, there is almost nothing here that qualifies as journalism. For one, the whole approach is difficult to reconcile with the code of practice of the Press Complaints Commission (PCC), which at least in principle binds journalists working for member organisations and which includes clauses on such matters as accuracy, privacy and the use of subterfuge. The code makes clear, for example, that it is not acceptable to employ a clandestine recording device on a 'fishing expedition' – in other words, when you don't have good grounds to expect you will gain a particular kind of evidence of a particular kind of wrongdoing. Though the paper made desperate efforts in court to create the impression that it had had such grounds, the judge would not credit them and indeed no reasonable person would have.

In a way, though, the terms of the code were the least of it. This may sound pious, but it is a simple fact that journalism has to be about truth. If a reporter is not trying to write about the world as he or she sincerely believes it to be, then the product is not journalism. It is fiction passing itself off as journalism. In this case the paper didn't get what it hoped for (the Sieg Heil) but relied instead on some other German words it didn't understand and did not bother to have translated. (German = Nazi to the *News of the World*.) The paper promised its informant £25,000 and then paid her £12,000 because it knew she could not hold it to its word. It threatened people with exposure if they did not cooperate, but in court denied this was blackmail. It presented its readers with an 'interview' which was nothing of the kind. Even in court it could not get its facts straight. The judge observed of the author of the supposed interview: '... his best recollection is so erratic and changeable that it would not be safe to place unqualified reliance on his evidence'. And yet for all the shameful conduct that was laid bare, no one at the paper was disciplined or reprimanded, let alone sacked. In other words, this is what the *News of the World* does.

More than anything, though, it is in their attitude to the public interest that the privacy invaders mark themselves out as different. The public interest is central because it is a sort of get-out-of-jail card for journalists, though it is actually recognised only grudgingly in law. An ethical journalist can justify telling a lie, or covertly recording a conversation, or trespassing if this act is done in the pursuit of the public interest, and even if he or she is found guilty of an offence, others will usually understand this as valid and will give their support. The public interest can literally keep a journalist out of jail, and it is not merely in the eye of the beholder. The Press Complaints Commission, for example, defines it as follows:

> The public interest includes, but is not confined to:
> i) Detecting or exposing crime or serious impropriety
> ii) Protecting public health and safety
> iii) Preventing the public from being misled by an action or statement of an individual or organisation

How did the *News of the World* justify publishing the Mosley story, which concerned legal sexual activity between consenting adults? Mosley's behaviour, the trial was told, was 'so debased, so depraved that the law will not offer it protection from disclosure'. The alleged Nazi elements of his activities were said to have mocked the Holocaust and, when combined with Mosley's family background, contributed to a 'disturbing situation' which was of 'legitimate public interest'. Colin Myler, the paper's editor, further claimed that exposure was justified because 'as the head of Formula One Mr Mosley is the figurehead for the sport. He's invited to the opening gala dinners, whether it's with princes, prime ministers, kings, queens and presidents'. And the paper also argued that the beating which took place during the session amounted to a form of assault which it was legitimate to expose, and that Mosley's relationship with the women amounted to illegal brothel-keeping.

Not only did the court reject every one of these arguments but it also exposed the cynicism with which they had been prepared. The assault argument, put forward only after Mosley sued, was dismissed by the judge as 'artificial' and 'verging on desperation'. The brothel-keeping charge, he noted, had been 'thought up' by the paper's lawyers, only to be 'abandoned' before the trial's end. As for the Nazi theme, it turned out to have no foundation in fact – and here the judge's remarks revealed just how a public interest defence works in the hands of privacy invaders. He said he was 'prepared to believe' that the paper's editors and reporters, 'on what they had seen, thought there was a Nazi element – not least because that is what they wanted to believe. Indeed they needed to believe this in order to forge the somewhat tenuous link between the claimant [Mosley] and his father's notorious activities more than half a century ago, and, secondly, to construct an arguable public interest defence ...'

There was no cool assessment of the evidence, therefore, and no measured calculation of whether this was really one of those rare cases where intrusion into someone's most private affairs could be justified because exposure makes the world a better place. This was about what they wanted and needed to believe if they were to publish – and they were determined to publish. In other words, the story comes first and then, as the judge put it, you 'construct an arguable public interest defence'. And if that defence doesn't work you try another, and another, and another. This is not how journalists behave. They don't 'think up' public interest cases which are 'artificial', and they don't allow themselves to believe something just because it suits them. They don't abuse the entire ethical structure just so they can get whatever it is they know or believe they know into print. Certainly they get things wrong sometimes and they make misjudgments, but their general aim is to act ethically, just as it is to act truthfully.

The suggestion that journalists are ethically driven often provokes sniggering, because many people believe the opposite. Yet journalists spend more of their time confronting and worrying about ethical questions than people in most other walks of life. Being accurate, balanced, fair and responsible while

Daily Express headline about the disappearance of Madeleine McCann, 10 September 2007
Credit: Jonathan Hordle/Rex Features

LY EXPRESS

EWSPAPER

www.express.co.uk

MONDAY SEPTEMBER 10, 2007 40p

parks to choose from in England, Scotland, Wales and the Isle of Wight

50

LIDAYS

from a 4 night midweek, a 3 night

nd family break or week long stays

FOR EVERY READER

Price per person, based on four sharing. Service charges may apply. Selected dates apply. Tokens collect. See Page 40

MADELEINE

'WE CAN PROV

PARENTS DI

uese police

matic new

idence

turning around a product that is acutely time-sensitive is demanding. You will not always agree with the decisions they make, but it is a simple fact that professional publications and professional journalists take these matters seriously though the procedures are often not formal. It is obvious, however, that no such scruples attended the preparation of the *News of the World*'s Mosley scoops, and it would be hard to exaggerate how far recklessness has damaged the name of journalism in recent years.

The coverage of the disappearance of Madeleine McCann in 2007, when a dozen national newspapers printed between them hundreds of grossly libellous stories on their front pages over a period of nearly a year, is probably the most shocking instance (though it was not a privacy issue). The *Express* papers were the worst offenders on that occasion, forced to pay a reported £550,000 in damages – and what soul-searching followed? What did the then editor of the *Daily Express*, Peter Hill, do to ensure it could not happen again? He famously told MPs: 'I have reprimanded myself.' Journalists tend to laugh or shrug at this but they should take it seriously, because with those words Hill was mocking what they do for a living.

In both motivation and method, the Mosley case demonstrates, journalism is distinct from the industry of privacy invasion. But the privacy invaders prefer to muddy the water. When the *News of the World* lost that case it announced that 'our press is less free today after this judgment' – appealing, by implication, to a noble British history and British tradition of press freedom. Now press freedom is an important matter and its history is certainly rich in noble deeds, but William Cobbett and John Wilkes did not suffer imprisonment and exile to enable journalists to bribe, bully and deceive their way into other people's bedrooms. Nor, if you forgive the anachronism, did they have in mind the sort of people who would illegally hack into the mobile phone messages of the famous on the off-chance they might learn something titillating. These martyrs in the cause of press freedom had some meaningful conception that the press needed to be free to serve the public interest, and they did not see the public interest merely as a smokescreen.

You may by now be thinking that this is all very precious, and wouldn't it be a dull world if we didn't have these naughty boys in the tabloids blowing raspberries and shaking things up? It's a comfortable attitude so long as you are not at risk of being a victim of the intrusion for which it is a cover, and so long as you don't care that innocent people suffer for it. But spare a thought for those of us who teach the journalists of the future. What are we supposed to tell them? 'Don't worry about ethics because, so long as only a minority of people suffer from what you do, the majority will thank you for making the world a more diverting place'? That is not a viable attitude.

The privacy invaders use another version of that argument. They suggest that they are journalists, but the anarchic, irreverent, pushy part of the business, keeping the rest on its toes and preventing complacency. Again this isn't viable. They don't keep journalism virtuous; they drag it down, routinely showing contempt for the kind of boundaries they demand to see enforced in every other part of society. When the *News of the World* was convicted of illegally breaching Max Mosley's privacy, it raised two fingers to the court, attacked the judge and the law and did nothing whatever to alter its habits. When the *Express* was caught libelling the McCanns, nobody was disciplined and nothing changed and, as we have seen, the editor mocked the idea that it should be otherwise. When Gordon Taylor, head of the Professional Footballers' Association, produced evidence in 2008 that his phone had been hacked by the *News of the World*, the paper paid him £700,000 to shut up and go away.

For the privacy intruders the water can never be muddy enough. We are told that celebrities collaborate in their own exposure and it's all part of the modern publicity industry. Often true, no doubt, but not always – and any journalist should be able to tell the difference between the person who wants to tell or sell a story and the person who has to be stalked, deceived and bullied for a story. We are told that public figures have an obligation to behave in certain ways because they are 'role models'. Among the many problems with this are that the standards are arbitrarily set by editors and inconsistently applied, simply because the test is not what is right or wrong but what will sell newspapers on a given day. And editors who live by such dictates (and rely on dubious means to get their stories) are surely the last people we should rely on to judge what is appropriate conduct and what is not. We are also told that this is all about power and privilege, that the protection of privacy is a confidence trick designed to conceal from us the wrongdoing of top people. This is a con trick in itself. It just happens that editors aren't usually interested in intruding upon the privacy of the poor, but when the time comes that they are – say in the case of victims of crime or with bereaved families – they often show no mercy. Rich or poor, they will stitch you up if it suits them.

Paul Dacre, the editor of the *Daily Mail*, has offered a different and curious defence. In a speech in 2008 he argued: '... if mass-circulation newspapers, which also devote considerable space to reporting and analysis of public affairs, don't have the freedom to write about scandal, I doubt whether they will retain their mass circulations with the obvious worrying implications for the democratic process'. This implies that professional intrusion into privacy is a price society has to pay if people are to be informed about things that are genuinely in the public interest. That can't be right. It is true that the *News of the World* carries coverage of public affairs, indeed it occasionally prints front-page stories which are genuinely in the public interest – its coverage of match-fixing in cricket was a case in point. But journalists know that every story has to stand on its own ethical merits. Because you have published one worthy story does not mean that in the next one you have a licence to intrude. That is like saying that if you get 20 stories right you are free to commit a libel in the 21st, providing the story helps to keep your paper afloat. If the *News of the World* is to survive, it should pay its way by reporting in the public interest, full stop.

Let us say, then, that we are going to make a distinction between journalism and intruding in people's privacy. Two questions immediately arise. First, where is the line between the two? And second, what difference does it make?

This is not simply a matter of drawing a line between tabloids and broadsheets, as they used to be, or between populars and qualities, as they were before that. In the first instance, we are identifying a kind of activity, but from there it is a short step to knowing who the people are who routinely engage in that activity, and which are the organisations that encourage, condone and trade by it. It is not all that complicated. The new non-journalist category, incidentally, will include some people not previously thought of as journalists, people like Glenn Mulcaire, Jonathan Rees and Steve Whittamore – private detectives who in their day were employed by the *News of the World* and who have all, incidentally, been convicted of crimes. Is this snobbish? Only if you believe there is something elitist about having ethical standards. Is it realistic? If we put aside the obfuscation, and make the effort to recognise these distinctive activities when we see them, yes. It really is not such an effort to tell the difference between those who want to inform and entertain and those who share the motivation of the former assistant news editor on the *News of the World* who told a colleague in 2002: 'This is what we do. ... We go out and destroy other people's lives.' And it could be argued that making the distinction might strengthen the hand of those people in the relevant organisations who want to behave ethically.

Will it make a difference? Certainly not in the sense that it will solve the privacy problem, and put an end to unjustified intrusion. That argument will run and run, and it is likely that no satisfactory boundaries will ever be fixed.

Moreover the intruders, who are resourceful, will find ways to shield at least some of what they do. But the distinction will help to clarify the debate by separating those participants who have no real interest in ethical conduct or the public interest from those who do. It will more clearly expose the interests of those who argue that that law which allows scrutiny of the activities of a corporation must also allow scrutiny of the private life of an individual. And it will surely lend extra weight to the demands of journalists to be free to do what is genuinely the work of journalism.

This is an urgent matter. Because of the serial horrors – McCann, Mosley, hacking – the demand for statutory regulation of the press is growing. The Press Complaints Commission has failed to shore up standards or to convince the public that the press is sincere in wanting to regulate itself. If journalists, for reasons of nostalgia, inertia, confusion or misplaced loyalty, choose to keep swimming with the privacy intruders, they may well drown with them. If they push themselves free, then there is a better chance that we will find ways of protecting the freedoms that are vital to journalism.

Most of all, though, a clearer distinction will benefit the reading public. The more distance that opens up between ethical journalism and professional intrusion into privacy, the more the public will understand what it is getting and what it can trust. And that is in the public interest. ❐

40(2): 35/45
DOI: 10.1177/0306422011410013
www.indexoncensorship.org

Brian Cathcart is professor of journalism at Kingston University and former media columnist at the *New Statesman*. He was a journalist at Reuters and the *Independent*. His books include *The Case of Stephen Lawrence* (Penguin). He is a regular contributor to www.indexoncensorship.org

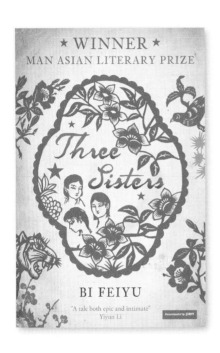

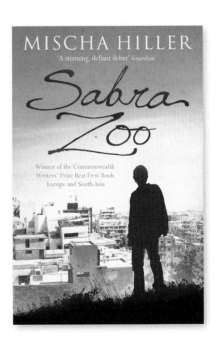

BALANCING ACTS

The British press loves to hate high court judge **Sir David Eady** for his judgments in privacy cases. He talks to **Joshua Rozenberg** about balancing rights

Where should we draw the line between personal privacy and freedom of expression? In England and Wales, such questions are left to the judges to decide. Parliament has chosen not to create a privacy law; no doubt because politicians of all parties have no wish to antagonise the media any more than is necessary. Even if there were legislation, it could not define all the subtle variants that occur in the real world. So it will always be up to judges to balance Article 8 of the European Convention on Human Rights, which requires respect for a person's private and family life, against Article 10, which protects freedom of expression.

That's certainly the view of Sir David Eady, and he should know. As the senior high court judge responsible for privacy and defamation work until recently and still a part of the specialist judicial team, Mr Justice Eady has decided several of the leading cases in this rapidly developing area of the law. Perhaps the best known of these is the claim that Max Mosley brought against the publishers of the *News of the World,* of which more anon.

Speaking to me over tea and cakes at the Royal Courts of Justice in London, Eady recalls that when Labour came to power in 1997 it had

Caroline of Monaco lawyer German Matthias Prinz presents replicas of photographs published in German magazines in the 1990s, 6 November 2003, Strasbourg, France
Credit: Olivier Morin/AFP/Getty Images

always intended the judges to develop a law of privacy. All that was needed was for the human rights convention to be incorporated into the domestic legal systems of the United Kingdom. Under the Human Rights Act 1998, which took effect in 2000, courts are required to 'take into account' decisions of the human rights court in Strasbourg when interpreting the convention.

'It's clear from Strasbourg jurisprudence that anything sexual – anything concerned with personal relationships – attracts protection under Article 8,' Eady says. 'And that's normally the subject matter we're concerned with, because the press is normally interested in footballers, sex and so on. The big question comes when you have to balance Article 8 against Article 10.'

As a rule, he explains, courts must apply the test in the Princess Caroline case, *von Hannover v Germany*, decided by the human rights court in 2004: the decisive factor is whether the publication contributes to 'a debate of general interest to society'. If the case is about a footballer having a fling, the answer is almost certainly that it doesn't.

One case in which Eady did have to strike a balance was *Lord Browne of Madingley v Associated Newspapers*, decided in 2007. The then chief executive of BP tried to stop his former partner from speaking to the *Mail on Sunday* about their four-year homosexual relationship. Browne resigned from BP immediately after the court of appeal disclosed that he had lied in court about the circumstances in which the two had met.

'Some of the subject-matter of the case was private,' says Eady. 'Some engaged the public interest or the interests of shareholders.' And so the media was permitted to report certain aspects of the case. 'But in most cases, public interest is not even argued, particularly at the preliminary stage. And there haven't been many trials.'

If there is a balance to be struck – perhaps because a claimant has forfeited his right to privacy – then the law demands what judges have described as an 'intense focus' on the comparative importance of the rights being claimed. There may be room for debate over whether a relationship is already in the public domain: is the relationship known, for example, only to those in an individual's workplace or more widely? It may be necessary to keep the claimant's identity private to protect the privacy of his lover or his children. Perhaps an innocent party's mental health might be jeopardised by disclosure. And circumstances may have changed between the granting of an injunction and the time the case comes to trial.

'It's not a precise art and you can't legislate for a precise outcome,' Eady says. It's inherent in a balancing exercise that different judges may reach different conclusions on whether the same couple are conducting their relationship in public or in private. You might say they have appeared together on so many occasions or at so many parties or public functions that this is no longer a private matter. But another judge might say: "Well, I think they've been fairly discreet about it".'

But he insists that judges do not decide privacy cases on the basis of their religious views or some moral code. What they're focusing on is the principles laid down in previous cases – in particular, the Strasbourg jurisprudence. If so much depends on a single judge's intense focus on the case, then perhaps we should pay more attention to the individual judges themselves. There was some concern that Eady, as the judge in charge of the Queen's Bench jury list until recently, was hearing too many privacy cases himself.

He points out that because privacy is derived from the law of confidence, which evolved as an equitable remedy, many privacy claims are brought in the Chancery division of the High Court – where Eady himself does not sit. The most recent example of this involves allegations of phone-tapping by the *News of the World*, a case being tried by Mr Justice Vos. Other important privacy issues are dealt with in the Family division.

But Eady acknowledges his own involvement in developing privacy law. 'It so happened that I was judge in charge of the list for several years and the practice was in those days that I never did anything else but the Queen's Bench list.' Although it's a large division, most of its judges are assigned to other work – criminal trials and appeals, for example, or judicial review – and so it was inevitable that a high proportion of the privacy cases would come before Eady.

Mr Justice Tugendhat, who succeeded Eady as judge in charge of the jury list, is doing a broader range of work. But media cases generally – not just privacy claims – still tend to come before the specialist judges if they are available: Tugendhat, Eady and now Mrs Justice Sharp. 'There's an increasing tendency towards specialisation among the judiciary and the "customers" like to get in front of a specialist judge if they can,' Eady explains. 'That tends to be the fashion of the day.'

Can litigants actually choose their judge? 'They make a request. And if it's a reasonable request then the listing office tries to co-operate.' What's not acceptable is to ask for a case not to be listed before a particular judge for no good reason.

Eady seems resigned to the fact that his decisions are going to be misunderstood and misreported in the press. In complicated cases, he may write a short summary of his decision for the benefit of reporters. But he would not wish to see judges or their communications office justifying decisions by way of a press release. He accepts that ill-informed media comment is something that goes with the territory. 'I think it's inevitable because the press are interested in the press's own affairs. So privacy and libel get much more coverage than personal injury, commercial cases or even public law, all of which are just as important if not more important.

'There are lots of judgments that have been criticised where it's quite apparent that people haven't read them. But there's nothing you can do about that: the press office aren't going to give them a spoonful of sugar to make it easier. And if they want to criticise the judgment, they will – whatever it says. But I don't really bother to read that stuff.'

He thinks again. 'I couldn't miss the Dacre stuff, obviously,' he adds, referring to a speech made by the editor of the *Daily Mail* to the Society of Editors conference in 2008. Paul Dacre had asserted that 'while London boasts scores of eminent judges, one man is given a virtual monopoly of all cases against the media enabling him to bring in a privacy law by the back door'. There had been more of the same criticism subsequently, Eady recalls. 'Essentially, the problem is that it misunderstands the function of a judge. It's presuming that a judge has some kind of political or personal agenda when all that he or she is doing is applying or interpreting the law, rightly or wrongly.'

Surely, judges are human and they are bound to be influenced by their personal views?

'Judges are human and they make mistakes,' Eady replies. 'But I think they make a pretty good fist at not being influenced by personal, political or religious views. So if you are saying that somebody should have their privacy maintained in relation to a certain type of lawful but unconventional conduct, that doesn't mean you go along with it or behave in that way yourself – or necessarily approve of it or have a view about it. If it's lawful conduct between consenting adults, that's it: it doesn't matter what your own personal views or inclinations may be.'

Eady is clearly referring to the Max Mosley case, which he decided in 2008. At that time, Mosley was head of motor-sport's governing body, the FIA. He established that the *News of the World* had breached his privacy by revealing that he enjoyed sado-masochistic sex sessions.

But the £60,000 damages Eady awarded Mosley was little consolation for the FIA boss. What Mosley would have preferred was a permanent injunction that prevented details of his sexual preferences from being revealed in the first place. Since he had kept them private, that application would almost certainly have been granted. But there was no application for such an order because Mosley had no idea that the *News of the World* was about to invade his privacy. The newspaper was not required to warn him in advance and it deliberately withheld the story from the edition that was available on the night before publication.

That's the gap in the law that Mosley tried to fill. He asked the European Court of Human Rights to rule that the lack of any requirement to notify a potential claimant before writing about his private life amounted to a breach of Article 8. In May 2011, his claim was dismissed, partly because of the 'chilling effect' that it would have had. But how significant would it be if Mosley had won and publishers had been required to warn people before writing about their private lives?

'I'm not sure it would be terribly significant', Eady says, 'because there are not that many cases where a newspaper is able to keep it that secret.

Former International Automobile Federation president Max Mosley leaves the European Court of Human Rights in Strasbourg, 11 January 2011
Credit: Vincent Kessler/Reuters

I genuinely don't have a personal view on whether it should or shouldn't happen but I can understand why Mosley is so keen about it.'

Surely it would have an impact on the media? Every time we wanted to disclose personal information about an individual, we would have to give the person concerned an opportunity to seek a court order blocking publication.

An injunction is by no means automatic, Eady insists, although the claimant stands a good chance of being granted an order for a few days, pending a full hearing. But the sort of case we are talking about is not one where the claimant would rush off to court without notifying the defendant newspaper. Since the publisher would have alerted the claimant in the first place, there is no reason why the newspaper should not be represented at the initial court hearing. And if there was a public interest in publication – because, to take a hypothetical example, the mental capacity of a judge, a minister or a surgeon was affected by an undisclosed brain tumour – then an injunction would be refused.

Sex and health are clearly areas that the law will protect in the absence of any over-riding public interest in disclosure. So are personal financial affairs. But what about other areas that an individual in a responsible position may wish to keep private, such as extreme political or religious views? Would the law prevent such views from being made public by a spouse?

'That's quite a difficult question to answer,' Eady admits. There may be no evidence that the individual's private views had ever affected the holder's public position. 'On the other hand, you might say that it's difficult to envisage how somebody who holds those views can be rational.'

Because the French burqa ban happens to be in the news on the day I am interviewing Eady, we discuss what would happen in the case of a strict Muslim who might not let his wife appear in public unless she wears a full veil.

'Does that necessarily mean that the person shouldn't be allowed to be a judge, or a teacher or whatever it might be? To what extent has he allowed those views to intrude on his decisions or conduct? It all depends on the circumstances.'

At some point, he continues, an individual's views may become so irrational that his judgment cannot be trusted on anything. 'I'd have considerable doubts about a flat-earther being a teacher, or a judge or a doctor.'

So would it have made any difference if there had been a Nazi element to Mosley's sado-masochistic activities?

'It might have done,' he admits. 'I didn't have to grapple with that in the end because I found that there wasn't. But if he had been mocking Holocaust victims – which was one of the allegations made in the *News of the World* – there would have been quite a powerful argument for saying that should have been revealed. He had, at that time, a role in the FIA, which involved dealing impartially with people of all creeds, races, colours and so on.'

It would, of course, have been possible for Mosley to have brought a libel action over the article, which was headlined F1 Boss has Sick Nazi Orgy with 5 Hookers. If the newspaper had sought to justify its allegation that there was a Nazi element to Mosley's role-play, that defence would have been dismissed by Eady on the facts that emerged at the privacy hearing.

'There is a close comparison between privacy and libel,' Eady tells me. 'They interlink because they're both part of the human personality – or, as they tend to call it in Strasbourg, human integrity. So one can see why Article 8 would have them both under its umbrella – although originally, of course, it didn't. It's a very recent development that libel has been brought in under Article 8 – not in the convention, obviously, but in case law.'

And that poses problems. In English law, the same set of facts may give rise to claims in either privacy or libel. A claimant may then choose how to proceed. Much may depend on whether he is seeking an interlocutory injunction – one that prevents publication pending a full hearing.

In libel, all that a defendant need do to resist such an injunction is to say he will prove that what he published was true – a test that goes back 120 years to the case of *Bonnard v Perryman*. 'That's not an answer in privacy, obviously,' explains Eady. 'The issue is not, "Is it true?" but "Is it your business?"'

In deciding whether to grant an injunction in a privacy case, the court must consider whether the claimant is likely to succeed when the case comes to trial. 'It's a much easier burden for a claimant to discharge in a privacy case than in a libel case because injunctions in libel cases are almost never granted.' Having said that, Eady mentions a recent exception. In *ZAM v CFW*, decided in March 2011, the high court granted an injunction on the basis that the claimant could not be fully compensated in damages for the injury to his reputation if the threatened libel – which was held to be clearly false – was published.

'Since Strasbourg now regards both privacy and libel as coming under the Article 8 umbrella, the question arises: is it any longer feasible, or sensible, or justifiable, in principle for having separate tests for interlocutory injunctions, depending on whether it's privacy or libel?'

Is that as far as it goes – or will we eventually see libel and privacy subsumed into one tort called protection of reputation or protection of personal integrity?

As the law now stands, there would be problems at the damages stage, Eady explains. 'One of the things you have got to be careful about is not to give a claimant an award of damages which represents restoration of reputation, so that he or she gets the benefit of suing for libel without having done so.'

At the time we are speaking, there is something of a media frenzy over 'super-injunctions' – court orders that ban reports of their own existence, at least temporarily. 'The classic example of this is of a threatening blackmailer, which is surprisingly common: I'm dealing with one at the moment and I can think of three or four this year. People who know somebody who's in the public eye and know something that they think is discreditable see the opportunity for making money. They're in touch with journalists who are ready to pay it.'

In those circumstances, the judge is likely to grant an injunction. But what happens if the potential blackmailer hears about it through the media before it is formally served on him? He would not be bound by it. 'There is a risk he'll go to the journalist, clinch the deal and then say, "You can't touch me".' Eady says those are 'classic circumstances' for the grant of a super-injunction.

Once the court order has been served on the blackmailer, there is no reason why its existence should not be reported. Indeed, the judgment Eady is writing appears a few days after we speak. *OPQ v BJM and CJM* is unusual because Eady granted an order of general effect – 'against the world' – banning publication of confidential information about the claimant on a permanent basis.

This is something of an innovation. But it has the same effect as a temporary injunction granted ahead of a full hearing. Under the so-called *Spycatcher* doctrine, such an order binds everyone who knows about it. But that restriction is thought to lapse once a case settles, as *OPQ v BJM* is about to do. Hence the need for a universal order – which is perfectly logical once you accept the fundamental principle that people are generally entitled to keep their private lives private.

'It's surprising how many injunctions do hold and how many are settled on private terms, fairly quickly,' Eady tells me. That includes cases where the press are defendants – 'because they recognise, on mature reflection, that there's no public interest argument and they're happy to get out of it'.

For his part, Eady seems to be in no hurry to get out of a job he clearly enjoys. But those judges who were appointed after February 1995 – including Eady and most of his serving colleagues – must retire when they reach the age of 70. That leaves Eady with less than two years to go. Still, with privacy developing as quickly as it is, it will be fascinating to see how far he can develop the law before he leaves the public stage and tries to regain the personal privacy that has eluded him on the bench. ❒

The interview with Sir David Eady took place on 11 April

40(2): 47/55
DOI: 10.1177/0306422011410270
www.indexoncensorship.org

Joshua Rozenberg is a leading commentator on the law and presents the popular BBC Radio 4 series *Law in Action*. His books include *Privacy and the Press* (Oxford University Press)

Photographers outside the Elysée Palace following the marriage of President Nicolas Sarkozy and Carla Bruni, Paris, France, February 2008
Credit: Sipa Press/Rex Features

D'ARTAGNAN'S TUNE

France's culture of privacy is being challenged in an unprecedented stand-off. **Natasha Lehrer** reports

The arrest of Dominique Strauss-Kahn in New York on 14 May has shone a spotlight on the private life of the man many believed would be president of France. One of the most powerful men in the world stands accused of attempted rape. France stands accused too – of turning a blind eye to the entitled, arrogant sexism of its political elite, and of fostering a journalistic culture that has long been complicit.

There are those in France who would have you believe that freedom of the press, like the notion of human rights itself, is a French invention. 'The free communication of ideas and opinions' was enshrined in the 1789 Declaration of the Rights of Man as 'one of the most precious of the rights of man. Every citizen may, accordingly, speak, write, and print with freedom' within the bounds of the law. Yet, like so many of those famous rights, it appears that in its spiritual home press freedom can be something of a chimera. As more and more damaging stories circulate about DSK, as Strauss-Kahn is known in France, French journalists are finding themselves called to account for the first time.

One of the elements that has historically limited journalistic freedom in France is the country's draconian privacy laws, which make some of the types of press intrusion that are so common in the UK and the US subject to legal proceedings. Whilst there are many who would acknowledge that limiting the kind of press intrusion that Britain's tabloids specialise in is surely not a bad thing, it has inevitably led to a climate where journalists self-censor and the public expresses profound scepticism regarding journalistic probity.

The origins of the protection of privacy in France can be traced back to the 19th century when French law started to develop personality rights, including the right to control one's image, though it was not until 1970 that a general right to respect for private life was added to the Civil Code (Article 9). This was modelled on Article 8 of the European Convention on Human Rights which, since its ratification by France in 1974, is now directly applicable in domestic law. In 1995, the right to privacy was given constitutional value in France by the Constitutional Court.

Under the 1970 law everyone, including those in the public eye, regardless of rank, birth, wealth and present or future role in society, is entitled to have his or her private life respected; where this is infringed, damages can be awarded and the offending publication may be seized, pulped and required to publish the judgment against it. However, there are instances where it has been recognised that different types of public interest may allow interference with the right to privacy; for example, the French media has been allowed to publish a list of the 'hundred wealthiest French people', with details of their wealth, on the grounds that it is in the public interest that the position of these individuals in the business world be known.

Protection of privacy not only covers the disclosure of details of an individual's private life but also the taking and publication of photographs of an individual without prior consent. In the case of an interview, an individual's photograph may not be published for a purpose or in a manner which differs from the one which was originally agreed or in order to distort the manner in which the interviewee has elected to project their image or express their opinion. Intrusion into someone's private life can also be a criminal offence; anyone found guilty is liable to a term of a year's imprisonment and/or a fine up to a maximum of €45,000.

Somewhat problematically, the notion of what constitutes 'private life' has never been legally defined, although it has been established that private life includes family life, love life, illness and medical records and private address. Or, as a judgment from 1970 put it, Article 9 protects 'the right to one's name, one's image, one's voice, one's intimacy, one's honour and reputation, one's own biography, and the right to have one's past transgressions forgotten'. (Such a law would be a dream for some British politicians, one suspects.) Nonetheless, over the years judgments have tended to decide that there is a legitimate right for the public to know about events relating to public figures such as a birth, a divorce and even family conflict.

The most infamous privacy case took place in 1996, following François Mitterrand's death from cancer, with the publication of a book by his doctor called *Le Grand Secret*. It was alleged by Mitterrand's family that the book, in giving a detailed account of the president's illness whilst he was still in office, was in breach not only of medical confidentiality but also of the president's right to privacy. Mitterrand's family obtained an injunction for the immediate suspension of the distribution of the book. In his appeal the book's author did not rely on the public interest argument but instead on his right to freedom of expression. In overturning the author's appeal the court took the view that details of the president's illness involved the most 'intimate' aspect of privacy. Given that the president himself had issued regular bulletins about his health, whilst never admitting to being ill with the cancer which later killed him, it has been argued that what actually prevailed in the court's decision, as the legal expert E Picard has observed, was 'the right of the subject of the invasion [of privacy] to reveal what he wishes about himself even if, as in this case, it was not the truth'. The ultimate decision

Mitterand family lawyer at a press conference following a ban on sales of Le Grand Secret *by the former president's doctor, 18 January 1996*
Credit: John Schults/Reuters

of the Cour de Cassation – France's highest civil court – upheld the family's right to suppress the book, in effect maintaining what might be seen as a long-standing French tradition of suppressing information in the interests of political expediency.

Mitterrand's other great secret was his illegitimate daughter Mazarine, born in 1974. Her existence was finally revealed – with the publication of a photograph in *Paris Match* – in 1994, six months before the end of his presidency. Mitterrand had gone to extraordinary lengths throughout his presidency, including extensive wiretapping of journalists (under the cover of anti-terrorism legislation), to keep Mazarine's existence out of the public eye. Ironically, given how many resources Mitterrand expended in keeping Mazarine's existence a secret, the eventual publication of the photograph caused far less of a scandal than the fact that details about his illness were kept secret even after his death.

There are those who claim that the French are growing less respectful of the private lives of their politicians and that a story such as Mazarine Mitterrand could no longer be kept secret. Coverage of Nicolas Sarkozy and Carla Bruni's relationship has certainly been occasionally less than entirely respectful and there are regular threats issued by Sarkozy to sue various journalists or newspapers for publishing unflattering stories about the two of them. On the other hand, the press was maintaining a cover for Socialist Party presidential candidate Segolène Royal and her partner and leader of the Socialist Party, François Hollande, as recently as 2007. *Le tout Paris* knew that the image that all was well in the Royal house of Hollande was pure fiction. The couple had been living apart for months, Hollande having left Royal for a political journalist. Yet not a whisper of their split was revealed in the media until Royal herself announced it, a month after the first round of the elections. Given their respective roles in French politics and the fact that an election campaign was being waged in which their relationship was a key element in the branding of the *parti socialiste*, it was hard to argue that it was not in the public interest to know that they were in fact in the throes of a rancorous separation (the couple never married but they were together for 30 years and the parents of four children).

The damages awarded against the media in cases of breach of privacy are too low to act as a deterrent, so it is pertinent to consider how it is that the media remain in such deference to the country's political elite. A long tradition of actual as well as self-censorship is certainly part of the problem. Even after the 1881 law on press freedom was passed, the 20th century witnessed several extended periods when emergency censorship was implemented, including during both world wars. 'Political officials seemed to feel they could not rule a country at war without it,' as Clyde Thogmartin puts it in *The National Daily Press of France* (1998). Throughout the 1950s censorship returned periodically as the Algerian crisis threatened to dethrone de Gaulle. Television broadcasting was overtly censored and manipulated up until the end of de Gaulle's presidency in 1969 – he could not tolerate a national broadcasting authority that was not in thrall to his politics, and under his aegis the media in general, and television in particular, was instrumentalised as an agenda-setting mechanism influencing news as much as cultural output.

With such a history of political meddling in a so-called free press it is hardly surprising that there is a deep-rooted suspicion of journalists in France. According to a 2010 survey conducted by the Catholic newspaper *Le Croix*, 66 per cent of the adult population expressed a lack of faith in journalistic independence, believing journalists to be unduly influenced by political pressure. 'The impression of collusion between journalists and government is firmly rooted in public opinion,' was the newspaper's conclusion. According to Pascal Riche, the editor-in-chief and one of the founders of the French news website Rue89, 'the press are seen as people trying to stir the mud, or as people who are close to power, eating with politicians, disconnected from the people'. In spite of fine rhetoric about the importance of a free press to the workings of democracy, journalistic culture in France sometimes seems still to be locked in the traditions of the ancien régime.

Such scepticism could be linked to the fact that France has traditionally had one of the lowest levels of newspaper readership in western Europe (although with the recent arrival of free newspapers, overall readership has seen a significant increase). Without significant government subvention – whether in tax breaks or actual subsidies – most French newspapers, apart from the free papers such as *Direct Matin* and *Direct Soir* which are paid for by the advertising that fills half of their pages, simply could not survive.

Under Nicolas Sarkozy's presidency, the issue of press freedom in France has become even more precarious than it has been historically, partly due to the fact that the president counts amongst his closest friends several of the country's most powerful media barons. In effect, with important exceptions, much of the French media is controlled by six powerful conglomerates, all of which are owned by close friends of the president. Martin Bouygues, owner of a telecoms company as well as France's most popular TV channel TF1, is Sarkozy's youngest son's godfather and was one of the witnesses at his wedding to Carla Bruni. Another witness was Bernard Arnault, who owns the Louis Vuitton group LVMH, which includes in its stable two economics magazines and Radio Classique. François Pinault, France's wealthiest man and owner of the newspaper *Le Point*, is another friend. Vincent Bolloré, who lent the president his jet and yacht for a much-criticised post-election holiday in 2007, is head of a family-owned company that launched the digital television channel Direct 8 in 2005 and, in 2006, the free daily newspaper *Direct Soir*. Arms manufacturer and proprietor of the media empire Hachette, Arnault Lagardère, calls Sarkozy 'a brother'; his stable includes *Paris Match*, *Elle* and *Le Journal de Dimanche*. Another friend and arms manufacturer is Serge Dassault, who bought *Le Figaro* in 2004 and was quoted as saying in a creepy echo of De Gaulle: 'There is some information that is more bad than good. And this puts at risk the commercial and industrial interests of our country.'

It wasn't long after Sarkozy came to power in May 2007 that alarm bells began to ring. Off the record breakfast meetings have taken place in the Elysée Palace, where members of the foreign press were harangued by the president himself for their less than flattering coverage of his presidency: 'He was literally waving his finger in my face,' one correspondent said. In 2005, even before Sarkozy got the top job, when he was interior minister and planning his presidential campaign, the editor of *Paris Match* (owned by his crony Arnault Laguardère) was fired after he ran a cover story showing Cecilia, Sarkozy's not yet ex-wife, in the arms of another man. A year after Sarkozy became president it was announced that in future the president would have the final say in the appointment of the head of French state TV, replacing the independent body that had hitherto had that responsibility. No one was surprised at the announcement in June 2010 that Laurent Solly, Sarkozy's former deputy election campaign manager, had been appointed as a director of TF1 (the television channel owned by Martin Bouygues).

There have been various episodes of intimidation of journalists, including the arrest and harassment of Vittorio de Filippis, former publisher of *Libération*, in December 2008 at the instruction of the investigating magistrate, to which Reporters Without Borders allude in their damning report on France in their 2010 press freedom index. By 2010, France's position on the annual index was, at 44, below that of Namibia, Jamaica, Tanzania, Mali and Ghana. A decade ago France was ranked in respectable 11th place; today only Italy keeps France from the dubious accolade of being ranked the lowest country for journalistic freedom in Western Europe. Reporters Without Borders' commentary makes sobering reading:

> There has been no progress in several countries where Reporters Without Borders pointed out problems. They include, above all, France and Italy, where events of the past year – violation of the protection of journalists' sources, the continuing concentration of media ownership, displays of contempt and impatience on the part of government officials towards journalists and their work, and judicial summonses – have confirmed their inability to reverse this trend.

In October, the issue of press manipulation took an even more ominous turn. A mysterious series of break-ins, during which computers were stolen, took place at the offices of various news outlets, both print and digital, all of which had expended considerable coverage investigating the Affaire Bettencourt.

The affair centres around claims that Liliane Bettencourt, the L'Oréal heiress and the wealthiest woman in France, was guilty of tax evasion and the (possibly linked) question of a substantial, and illegal, donation to Sarkozy's presidential campaign. There is an ongoing investigation into the allegations. In March 2007, a former Bettencourt accountant called Claire Thibout alleged that Eric Woerth, head of Sarkozy's election campaign funding, had been given €150,000 specifically for the campaign; donations by individuals to a presidential campaign cannot exceed €4,600. The allegations, originally made during a police interview with Thibout and subsequently published by Mediapart, included startling claims that several unnamed politicians were in the habit of passing by the Bettencourt mansion in Paris to pick up large quantities of cash in unmarked envelopes. Secret recordings made by Bettencourt's butler reveal that Woerth's name came up frequently in the Bettencourt household; it also emerged that his wife had been employed as a financial advisor overseeing various aspects of the heiress's €17bn fortune.

Both Woerth and the government issued strenuous denials of any nefarious or illegal involvement in the Bettencourt affair. As the story gathered steam in October, the government was also accused of intimidating the press, including *Le Monde*, *Le Point*, and the digital news outlets Rue89 and Mediapart, for their part in revealing unpalatable details of Woerth's alleged involvement in the run-up to the presidential election in 2007. (Rue89 was set up by a group of former *Libération* journalists and Mediapart by Edwy Plenel, former editor of *Le Monde*, who, coincidentally, was one of the victims in the Mitterand wiretapping scandal 20 years earlier for his part in investigating the Rainbow Warrior story, amongst others). Earlier this year, both Woerth's home and the headquarters of the ruling UMP party were searched by investigators.

In November 2010, *Le Canard Enchaîné*, France's renowned, redoubtable and fiercely independent weekly satirical newspaper, alleged that the president had personally ordered the head of the French Internal Intelligence Service (DCRI), Bernard Squarcini, to spy on journalists investigating corruption under Sarkozy's regime.

According to the *Canard*, a meeting was held in September 2009 with Sarkozy's then chief of staff (now minister of the interior) Claude Guéant, a member of François Fillon's cabinet and an unnamed representative of Sarkozy, to try to determine a way to get around a 1991 law which forbids telecoms companies to hand over telephone records to the police. The article went on to claim that an agreement was made between the president, the prime minister and the police to overrule this particular interdiction, in the

Outgoing Labour Minister Eric Woerth leaves the presidential Elysée Palace days after a cabinet reshuffle, 18 November 2010
Credit: Lionel Bonaventure/AFP/Getty

'interest of the state'. Furthermore, according to the *Canard*, in an alarming instance of Orwellian manipulation, the president appointed what the newspaper described as a more 'accommodating' new head of the independent organisation that monitors state surveillance, the CNCIS, in October 2009. The new director, Hervé Pelletier, agreed to adopt the new interpretation of the law on the instructions of the Elysée in January 2010. Since then the police have been able to view detailed telephone records of journalists with impunity, without authorisation. The *Canard* has also claimed that First Lady Carla Bruni-Sarkozy was given access to the intelligence and police reports. In a further development in May, a French court ruled that a prosecutor acted illegally when he allowed the police to examine the phone records of two *Le Monde* reporters covering the Bettencourt story.

Meanwhile, Bernard Squarcini, head of the DCRI (French Internal Intelligence Agency), announced in November 2010 that he was suing for defamation; not to be outdone, in the same month Claude Guéant decided to sue Mediapart for defamation after the site explicitly claimed that he was personally responsible for an orchestrated espionage campaign against it. Amongst other allegations, two Mediapart journalists claim to have been pursued using GPS technology, for which the delightful neologism *géolocalisation* has been coined. The case is set to be heard in October.

Mediapart editor Edwy Plenel's response to the defamation suit is worth quoting at length:

> In this legal battle, Claude Guéant cannot claim to be acting on his own behalf. The best proof that he is no more than the French president's stand-in is that, contrary to the suit he is filing against us, we are unable to respond in kind. The astounding ruling recently taken by the Paris prosecutor ... extends the immunity from legal pursuit accorded to a sitting president 'to the acts carried out in the name of the presidency by his staff'.
>
> If this trial does go ahead, it will highlight the absurd 'kingdom' that the republic of France has become under this presidency. A 'kingdom' in which the prince's servants are allowed to prosecute journalists, yet which protects them from the citizens that we are. In another period when democratic values receded, during the 1950s at the time of the Algerian War, French writer and winner of the Nobel Prize for literature François Mauriac (1885–1970), writing his column in *L'Express* had these words, which inspire us still: 'I doubt that the press can be guilty of a crime of indiscretion. But the crime of silence does exist. When the day comes to settle scores, we will not be accused of having spoken out but rather for having kept quiet.'

Explaining why he decided to pursue Mediapart, Guéant told the *Journal de Dimanche*, 'You can't let people get away saying whatever they want, there are limits ... this assertion of such a stain on my character could become enormous.' Squarcini has said that the allegations are a strategy to 'destabilise the boutique (sic) at a moment when the terrorist threat is stronger than it has ever been'.

As diplomats and politicians the world over know to their cost, in these days of the internet and WikiLeaks it is increasingly difficult to keep secrets. In France, Sarkozy might have traditional media in his domain, with much of the national press and television channels in the hands of six musketeers dancing to D'Artagnan's tune, but as Plenel's robust 'J'accuse' suggests, the new internet media outlets are proving less easy to control. ❐

40(2): 56/66
DOI: 10.1177/0306422011410123
www.indexoncensorship.org

Natasha Lehrer is a freelance writer and editor based in Paris. Former deputy editor of the *Jewish Quarterly*, she is the editor of *Beyond Belief*, Index on Censorship's new case study on censorship

FOYLES
FOR BOOKS
'LADY C'
SOLD OUT
IN STOCK AGAIN
TOMORROW

MEET THE TROLLS

A loose community of anarchic and anonymous people is testing the limits of free speech on the internet. **Whitney Phillips** interviews one of them

In 2008 I began researching trolling subcultures on 4chan, the notorious internet messageboard and a hotbed of anonymous trolling activity; and Facebook, a veritable smorgasbord of trollable – or as trolls would say, 'exploitable' – content. Over the course of my project I have found that, while hardly a monolithic or clearly homogeneous group, most trolls meet the following basic profile: they self-identify as trolls, tend to be intelligent, are playful and mischievous and wildly antagonistic. Additionally, most trolls choose to remain anonymous and are dismissive of, if not actively resistant towards, calls for greater online transparency (particularly as articulated by Facebook's CEO Mark Zuckerberg, who told *Wired* magazine that he wants to create an online environment that encourages sharing). Indeed, to a troll, privacy and freedom are nearly synonymous, making perceived violations of privacy – both at the federal and local/platform level – tantamount to tyranny. That is, something to rail against. In terms of behaviour, trolling ranges from the vaguely distasteful to the borderline illegal: trolls taunt unsuspecting targets with seemingly racist, seemingly sexist and/or seemingly homophobic language; post shocking imagery, including pornography and gore, in order to derail conversation; and flood discussion threads with non sequiturs or grotesque distortions of other users' positions.

In short, trolls deliberately court controversial and transgressive humour. They do so to garner what many trolls refer to as 'lulz', a particular kind of aggressive, morally ambiguous laughter indicating the infliction of emotional distress. To the troll, the precise nature of this distress is secondary, if not downright inconsequential, to their enjoyment of its effects. In my experience, trolls are as likely to attack members of the Westboro Baptist Church (aka the 'God Hates Fags' church) as they are to torment gay rights activists, and would harass members of the KKK just as quickly as they would post racist messages on the National Association for the Advancement of Colored People's website. Put very simply, trolls are equal-opportunity offenders, primarily interested in lulz; this is what trolls refer to as 'the game'.

Paradoxically, then, trolling is both real and pretend, both playful and malicious. It is real to those who stand to lose and a game to those who stand to win – trolls themselves rarely have any personal investment in the things they do and say. In this sense, trolling is, and is designed to be, inherently one-sided. Trolls give themselves a choice (whether or not to participate, whether or not to take the things they say seriously), but they do not extend that choice to their targets. If they do, it's no longer trolling. Thus, if trolling is unethical, it's not because trolls mean what they say – it's because they don't.

The legal question is another matter entirely. In the US, trolling is, for the time being, protected by the First Amendment. More and more frequently, however – in both America and in Britain – trolling is equated with 'cyberbullying' (a problematic term in itself) and therefore risks being legally categorised as fighting words (an offence in the US) and/or outright harassment. In Australia, several trolls have been arrested under the country's rather draconian speech codes. Whether or not one regards trolling as morally or politically distasteful, the impulse to silence trolls embodies the brewing fight within and between governments regarding the perceived necessity for online censorship.

Early in my research, I was introduced to a prolific and particularly successful troll I would eventually come to know as Paulie Socash (obviously, not his real name). My relationship with Paulie is strictly virtual; though we have worked together for nearly two years, we have never met face to face and probably never will. The following interview was conducted over Facebook private message (our primary means of communication) and provides one perspective on trolls' behaviour. As Paulie argues, trolling may not be explicitly or traditionally political, but it is predicated on resistance to all forms of authority – placing trolling squarely at the centre of emergent debates surrounding online censorship.

Whitney Phillips: How did you get involved in trolling?

Paulie Socash: For me it was political discussion boards around 2002, especially those with a strong element concerned with 9/11 and its repercussions on national and international politics. It was an easy thing since I was already a participant in a few of these as myself (or the constructed online persona I projected of myself, really), but I decided to create a few alternate personas on these boards to target specific members who happened to be annoying or overly earnest (9/11 'truthers' and various hippie peacenik types for the most part). In other words, people that the real me persona would consider arguing with but knew it wasn't worth the time and effort to try a rational engagement – it was better, more entertaining, to make them mad through nonsensical postings, shock, or distorting their positions.

Content and style-wise, I followed the lead of other trolls I saw working those boards, but there was not really a hub to meet and discuss trolling or co-ordinate things I was aware of, which is quite different from today.

Whitney Phillips: How regularly do you do it and how do you decide where and how you're going to be active?

Paulie Socash: Like many trolls, I work in spurts of activity and often take breaks for weeks or months. Mostly at this point, I decide to troll when there is an event that is important, breaking news to a certain group – something people get invested in spending time following online. And the decision to troll is really a function of audience size times individual investment. So the Japanese earthquake and tsunami would be a major event with a huge online audience of people slightly to moderately invested (mostly sympathetic but less likely to spend hours every day on it), but the revelation of an animal abuse video and the subsequent attempts to identify the suspects would lead to a smaller grouping of people with a very strong investment (ie animal rights folks who spend every waking moment online trying to 'solve' the case). I'll stick with the specific thing for a while until it burns out and interest is lost or moderators wherever I'm trolling delete everything and ban all profiles.

Whitney Phillips: Do you see yourself as belonging to a group or community? If so, how would you characterise that community? What's its purpose?

Paulie Socash: To an extent, yes. But the community is very fluid – people come and go and return. And I'm not talking here about anyone who has ever trolled something for a few days or posts on 4chan. The community I see as my own is made up of trolls who have been at this for a while and take their anonymity seriously – we troll new, sloppy trolls as well (often by showing how unanonymous they are), by the way. Within this community there's a constant joking back and forth about outing each other, and the decision to drop even the slightest hint about who one is in real life is taken seriously.

Despite the upsides for trolls of a network (which I won't get into here), communities based on trolling are kind of a liability to trolls. If the point is to troll and remain anonymous, the more one socialises and lets out who one is outside of trolling, the more one undermines that purpose. People tend to actively troll less and let down their guard about personal info.

The purpose of the community ... I guess is to exchange ideas and techniques, and to plan co-ordinated trolling. The underlying philosophical purpose or shared goal, anyway, would be to disrupt people's rosy vision of the internet as their own personal emotional safe place that serves as a proxy for real-life interactions they are lacking (ie going online to demonstrate one's grief over a public disaster like Japan with total strangers who have no real connection to the event). This latter point can be said of trolls, too. There's a kind of interaction, in-your-face and disrespectful, that trolls would like to but can't do in real life (for various reasons), so they do it online.

Whitney Phillips: Why is it necessary to be anonymous? Is anonymity important for free expression?

Paulie Socash: Anonymity is critical, in my opinion. It allows one to freely state unpopular positions (whether one's own or not) without repercussions from those who think saying mean things should result in death threats or vigilante action. An open dialogue needs the fringes and radical elements, even when they are satirical, like *A Modest Proposal* [a satirical essay written and published anonymously by Jonathan Swift in 1729, proposing that Irish children be sold as food], which was, to an extent, trolling and just happened to be published anonymously.

Anonymous trolling also can act as a check for unexamined, poorly articulated examples of free expression. People who post foolish, unwise things online are certainly free to do so, but anonymous trolling allows for them to be called out and made to defend their positions in ways not always possible otherwise thanks to assumptions of a polite society (and, yes, I realise the paradox here in that trolls absolve themselves from such ownership of their words).

Whitney Phillips: How does your online activity relate to free expression? Do you regard yourself as a champion of free speech?

Paulie Socash: While I certainly take advantage of and support free expression in the abstract, I'm not a 'champion' of people actually engaging in free speech online, especially the entitled, solipsistic nonsense the internet (and especially Facebook) is full of. Personally, I'd like people to do a lot less of expressing their opinions and emotions online – it's pathetic, to be honest. People should find better outlets for these things than a Facebook page where some billionaires are making money hand over fist off people's feigned grief and involvement in some event or cause.

What trolls do, however, is push the envelope for what speech should be protected speech. Given the recent prosecution of trolls in places like Australia, what the US legislators and courts decide to do about online speech that pushes the boundaries is very important.

Whitney Phillips: It's my understanding that trolls go some way to protect their identity and their privacy. Do you see anything contradictory about occasions where you or others may invade people's privacy as part of your trolling activity?

Paulie Socash: The internet is not a private place, especially not Facebook. Just ask Mark Zuckerberg. That people think it is or should be is part of the many problems of our society's thinking about online communication. It is a public space and people should behave as such and not expect it to be all backpatting and flowers.

Whitney Phillips: Is there a moral/ethical component to trolling activities? Do you see yourself as protecting causes or individuals?

Paulie Socash: I can't speak for all trolls on this, but most have some lines they won't cross and things they take special interest in. For the most

Jonathan Swift: the first troll?
Illustration by Grandville from Gulliver's Travels, *1726*
Credit: INTERFOTO/Alamy

part, I'd say trolls are supporters of unfettered free speech and public access to everything (this goes along with filesharing and hacking and the like).

Whitney Phillips: Do you use other forums apart from Facebook? Are you active on 4chan?

Paulie Socash: I rarely go to 4chan. It's a timesink and not really fun to troll since most everyone there is in some way trolling (badly, usually). It's for people new to trolling or interested in producing variations on old themes, or waiting around for nude pictures to be posted. I'd say most long-term trolls are pretty dismissive of the site as a whole and, though it has its uses at times, it certainly isn't set up as a place for a community of people (or trolls) to plan or talk in depth about anything.

Whitney Phillips: Is trolling 'political'?

Paulie Socash: Many to most trolls claim that there is no moral/ethical/political component to their trolling – if it has one of these, then it isn't 'actual' trolling but so-called 'moral-faggotry'. This is obtuse, look-at-how-bad-I-am one-upsmanship and mostly false. All trolling has a political component and 99 per cent of trolls have some ethical/moral limits (for example, posting actual child porn is a line most will not cross for reasons beyond legal repercussion). The thing here is that repeated and predictable positions with respect to any issue reflect a lack of creativity or a set position that makes a troll very much like his targets. It is, after all, earnestness and self-righteousness that are the best things to attack when trolling, so having set positions of one's own is a problem. Most trolls just avoid topics they aren't willing to troll.

The bigger issue is whether the act of trolling represents a political action regardless of the individual's intent. I'd say yes in the same way I'd say yes about graffiti or hacking or other behaviours that disrupt the expected flow of everyday life (in real life or online). It is a privileged group that can troll, but they/we are pushing back against status quo expectations of decorum because we can. We despise the smugness and arrogance of the average internet user or entrepreneur, but most of us also realise the real irony that every thing we do drops more pennies in the pockets of those who control the actual virtual spaces. Honestly, Mark Zuckerberg has made millions *because* of trolls.

Whitney Phillips: Speaking of Facebook, what can you tell me about Facebook memorial page trolling?

Paulie Socash: The biggest media thing/moral panic related to trolling over the past year or so has been memorial pages for dead people on Facebook, usually those for dead *white* teenagers to 20-somethings. When these get trolled, a huge outcry follows from the thousands of people who obsessively watch the pages and then the media gets things wrong and makes a big stink. People are shocked that people could be so low as to say mean things about dead kids to their families or whatever.

The reality of this is simple: the vast majority of those who get large memorial pages on Facebook are cute little kids (Jamie Bulger) or pretty young ladies (Jenni-Lyn Watson, Chelsea King) or useful pawns for a cause (Tyler Clementi and other gay suicides). These memorial pages are decidedly *not* a place for friends and family to grieve (family and friends should be grieving together in private like normal people). In reality, these are havens for 'grief tourists': people who substitute online emotions and declarations of solidarity for real emotional relationships and friendship. Most memorial pages are not set up by friends or family; they are created by people who are too involved with the stories they read online or see on the news - people who derive some sense of self-importance and worth from being seen to care by strangers.

There are of course exceptions to this. There are indeed memorial pages set up by family that get trolled because your average user is too ignorant of the controls of the page given to them by Facebook (and internet culture in general) to deal with trolling. In some trolls' eyes, these people are asking for it for being ignorant. The other end of the spectrum is memorial pages actually made by trolls to draw in grief tourists – I won't say much about this, but the Jenni-Lyn Watson page was a prime example.

Whitney Phillips: How would you respond to the assertion that trolling creates a hostile space – or feeds into and replicates an existent hostile culture – for minority groups? What about the assertion that trolling is hate speech or harassment and therefore should be subject to existent legal restrictions? Should the current legal criteria of hate speech and harassment ever apply to online behaviours?

Paulie Socash: Hate crime legislation is stupid . . . as is hate speech, at least when prosecuted by governments for public spheres for adults (I obviously see the purpose in specific environments like a school that already have a ton of exceptions to free speech, but those aren't quite 'laws'). Seriously, if someone kills another person, isn't that always a hate crime? Someone should do an extra life sentence for murder because they chose to target someone who is gay, black, Hispanic, white (oh, they don't prosecute for that)? What about if the person murdered was a hippie, or a junkie, or a hobo, or a redhead? Does that count? Or how about rape? Isn't rape always a hate crime already? It's absurd that we even have these laws.

While there are exceptions to public free speech here in the US (specifically the 'fighting words' exception that allows me to justifiably hit someone talking trash about me), prosecutions or enhancements based on supposed intent, especially those online, are positively Orwellian. The claim that there is any element of trolling that causes someone to be trapped and bullied and subjected to a hostile environment is outright ridiculous. You can log out of the *public* forum you are engaged in. You can defriend, block, retaliate, or whatever those who are obviously not being nice to you online. It isn't like getting beat up or picked on while walking to the bus stop because you always have an element of control not present in real life situations – a logoff. The claim about kids online being naïve or otherwise easy targets is lame – where are the parents and their responsibility in all this? There's a good reason that Lori Drew [indicted in case of 'cyberbullying' a 13-year-old girl who committed suicide] was acquitted, and that went way beyond just trolling since she had a real life motive, apparently. The real question to ask with respect to teen suicides due to so-called 'cyberbullying' is why kids today are so likely to kill themselves over it. ❒

40(2): 68/76
DOI: 10.1177/0306422011409641
www.indexoncensorship.org

Whitney Phillips is currently completing her PhD thesis on internet trolling at the University of Oregon

A woman bids farewell to Google's internet search engine in China following the company's decision to move the service to Hong Kong, 23 March 2010
Credit: Jason Lee/Reuters

PRIVATE LIVES

Google's chief privacy counsel **Peter Fleischer** talks to Index about the challenges for free speech online

Last year, Google, the US internet giant, clocked up revenues of $29bn and profits of $8.5bn, mostly through delivering more than 65 per cent of the world's internet searches. It processes over one billion search requests every day through its one million servers in data centres around the world. Is it any wonder then that the company finds itself at the heart of the debate about privacy on the internet, a debate which is increasingly being played out in the courts worldwide and in the actions of a growing number of governments who would like access to the data Google holds on their citizens?

Google likes to portray itself as a champion of free speech and a safe pair of hands whose users can trust to protect their privacy: it is one of Index on Censorship's funders and partners. However, both politics and commerce have highlighted intrinsic tensions. Some may be of the company's own making, for example when Google innovations breach citizens' privacy, as has happened on more than one occasion over the past year. But others are down to the fact that international law has not kept up with the technological revolution of the past decade, with both issues bumping up against human rights legislation in Europe and political unrest in other parts of the world.

This year alone Google has had to challenge Spain's data watchdog over claims that the search engine invades personal privacy. The Spanish regulator had told Google to delete links to websites that contain personal information. Two months later, in France, the privacy watchdog fined the company for accidentally collecting and storing data through its Street View cars. This is the first time the company has been fined for a privacy violation. It escaped a fine in the UK, Spain, Italy, Australia, Hong Kong and the US in 2010 for the same breach. Probably its most embarrassing failure to protect user privacy, though, was during the roll-out of its Buzz social network, in 2010, when users found personal details, including email contacts, had been disclosed without adequate warning.

Last year, Peter Fleischer was one of three Google executives found guilty in Italy of violating privacy law, after a video was posted on Google Video in which an autistic teenager was bullied. All three were given six-month suspended sentences. The case created an outcry, raising serious questions for online freedom and the liability of internet companies.

Meanwhile, elsewhere on the global stage, one of the company's biggest headaches has come from China, where its annual revenues are estimated at between $200m to $600m. Google came in for a lot of criticism in 2005, when it first made a deal with the Chinese government that allowed it to set up shop there, because of its concessions on censoring what Chinese users could access. Its argument at the time was that some internet access was better than none.

Five years later Google announced it was no longer willing to censor search results in China and moved its search service to Hong Kong. So now the company no longer censors its Chinese users; unfortunately, the Chinese government has the technical ability to continue to block what it doesn't want its citizens to see.

Earlier this year the company announced that it would not be introducing its instant messaging service, Google Talk, into Iran as it was worried that it would not be secure enough and might put Iranian citizens at risk from their government. This begs the question about how benign the governments are in the rest of the world where the service is available.

But is it fair to expect Google to be a global policeman, or to blame it for letting its commercial interests sometimes compromise its concerns over privacy? The company would argue that when human rights clash with freedom of expression, or when governments put it under pressure to help them spy on or censor their citizens, it needs support from an integrated, strong international legal framework; that the ethical and political issues at stake are far bigger than any one company can deal with. Both Europe and the US are currently considering new privacy legislation, including the controversial 'right to be forgotten', which will allow users to withdraw their consent to sharing their data. *Caroline Palmer*

Index: One of the big issues you face is: if there is to be free speech online, does that mean that we have to sacrifice some aspect of our privacy? The European Commission is talking about introducing a right to be forgotten. There's also an ongoing case in Spain where Google, so far as I understand it, is currently challenging demands that it delete links to certain websites.

Peter Fleischer: First let's separate out a couple of different categories of speech online and how it impacts privacy and the right to be forgotten. The first and easiest case is: if I publish something myself, should I have a right to delete it again? And I think the answer is clearly 'yes'. That doesn't implicate censorship. It's unproblematic.

Where it becomes harder is where, in the name of privacy, or in the name of the right to be forgotten, a person wants to prevent someone else, a third party, from publishing information about himself or herself. The cases that we have in Spain are an example of this debate, but just to make it real, in Spain there are almost a hundred cases that have been

A Google Street View camera, part of the company's online mapping initiative, has met with privacy concerns from several governments, including those of Canada, Spain and the UK. London, 2008
Credit: Bill Brand/Alamy

brought against Google the search engine by the Spanish data protection authority because various institutions in Spain published information. I'm thinking about newspapers and the Spanish official government journal that individual Spanish people want to have deleted from the Google search index.

To give you a real example, there was an article published in *El País* about a cosmetic surgeon in Spain who was accused of medical malpractice. He filed a lawsuit with the Spanish data protection authority, asking them to force Google to remove a link to the *El País* article about this case. That is not the right to be forgotten as such, because no one is disputing the right of *El País* to publish this article, or for it to remain online, but it's an attempt to use the search engine as a way to make it harder to find, and that's why we're opposing that. It's not strictly speaking the right to be forgotten, it's more about trying to make content that is legally published harder to find. In practice it kind of works out the same way though. So we don't want the search engine, which ultimately is just an index of legitimate legal third party content on the web, to be used as a tool of censorship. If a court held that the original content was illegal, that's a completely different case. We would remove it from our index as well. But nobody is claiming that – this is legitimate, legal and in fact, true content on the web.

You asked the question much more philosophically, and I'll sort of start philosophically as well. I mean, privacy has never been an absolute. Privacy has always been a balance of interests. We do not as individuals live alone in a cave in the woods. We live in a society. There's always been an exchange of information about ourselves. Some of it is intentional and voluntary; some of it is just necessary and obvious in the society in which we live. Privacy has always been about striking the right balance between an individual's desire to keep some things about themselves private and the legitimate interests of society to share information in other contexts.

Those are the ways we see these privacy debates come up over and over again. The technological revolution on the internet means that more information is coming online, so the question about where to strike the right balance is being republished over and over, and that's why we're seeing these privacy debates. In many of the cases we did see a conflict between a person's desire to keep information private, and someone else's desire to talk about them, freedom of expression, to learn about them, to read about them, and that conflict is real, and I think we should discuss those cases because it puts two principles in conflict and lines have to be drawn and decisions have to be made.

Index: What's your feeling about the kinds of laws that are being put on the table at the moment? A privacy law in the United States, as well as a law being proposed by the European Commission. Do you think that governments are addressing it with a full understanding of how workable these kinds of laws might be? Or do you have a feeling there's a backlash at the moment and an attempt to control the internet?

Peter Fleischer: There's always been a debate about how to write privacy laws, and privacy is a very hard thing to write a law about, because it is precisely about balance of interests, about conflicting interests, conflicting principles, and it's about regulating something that is very hard to define, namely 'what is personal data?' So it's always been a challenge. It's true that challenge is becoming harder in the age of the internet, for several reasons. One is, there's a lot more data online. It's also true that data is moving around the planet much faster than was ever true in the past. That's the fundamental nature of the internet. It's also that data on the internet tends not to disappear over time, so all of those factors mean that privacy today is becoming more acute. I think those are the reasons why we're seeing governments about the world struggle with how to write or update privacy laws.

In Europe, as you know, we've had horizontal general data protection laws on the books since 1995. The question is how we update them for the age of the internet and that's what's going on right now and the European Commission is expected to publish its proposals about how to update those fundamental laws in the next, let's say, roughly six months. In the US, there've been literally hundreds and hundreds of what we call 'sectoral privacy laws' in specific areas, but there has not been a horizontal federal privacy law across all fields like the way we have it in Europe, and that's one of the things that's been proposed in the US. So there has never been a time – I've been in this field for 20 years – when there's been more government focus on how to write and expand privacy laws than there is now, and I think that is a direct reflection of the broader trends that we have been talking about.

Now when you say: 'How are governments doing all this?' Well, these are really tough issues, what I would almost call technocratic issues. Just how do you make the mechanics of data protection work better in the modern age and, as a practitioner in the field, I care a lot about those, but they just go to process and form filling and how do you make the whole stuff work better?

But some of them go to much harder issues that are essentially philosophical, ideological questions, and the right to be forgotten is one of those.

It's like, where do you, as a government, want to draw the line between sometimes competing principles, right? What I'm trying to do is to define the questions in a way that helps policy makers make a decision. But as long as we're confused, or just too general about what we mean, it's very hard to have a thoughtful policy discussion. It's also true that even if you have a policy discussion you need to think about what is implementable, in the real world, and what will the effects be in the real world.

So let's say that you passed a law in, let's take a country like Germany, and it says after a certain period of time all references to someone's criminal convictions should be deleted. Now, you can understand why the country created a law like that – they wanted to give people a fresh start. They don't want them to be trailed throughout their lives with a criminal conviction. It makes it harder for them to rent an apartment, or get a new job or things like that. And even though we understand that, on the other hand, how do you implement that online? Does that mean that you are going back and deleting historical archives of newspapers that might have reported the conviction? I don't know. Is that what we want? Even if you did that in Germany, it has no impact outside of Germany, right? So if the same report appeared in a non-German newspaper, let's say in France or the US, it's still out there. So those are the kind of really practical implementation questions that I think it's important to wrestle with.

Index: So how does a country like Germany propose a law like that, that is essentially nonsensical? What does that say about the way that they're thinking about privacy?

Peter Fleischer: Well, I don't want to call it 'nonsensical'. What I'm saying is that they pass a law that is thoughtful and is human in what they're trying to do, but what I'm just saying is, in the real world will it accomplish what they're trying to do? And one of the things that I try to recommend in these policy debates is to think about both how it will play out in the real world, and also how does it play out internationally.

The internet is global, and because the architecture of the internet is such that data just doesn't start and stop at national borders, we have to think globally, and a lot of these policymakers understandably come to these issues from a very national perspective. You're a local politician elected in a particular country and you think it's my job to pass a law in my country. It makes the task of policymaking harder because you not only have to decide in your country, you have to achieve more of an

Bill Echikson, senior manager of communications of Google Inc, speaks to the media after an Italian court convicted three Google executives for privacy violations, Milan, 24 February 2010
Credit: Paolo Bona/Reuters

international consensus, but that's just the nature of the game now and that's one of the reasons that we have been advocating for many years that people should think about privacy regulation in a global context. We should be thinking about global privacy standards, for example, and I've been advocating them personally for many years and I think that it's growing into a very large consensus that in the long run that is the right way forward in Europe. I think it's widely understood that we need to have harmonised data protection law across all of Europe – that individual country laws just won't work anymore – and that's why everyone's waiting for the Commission's proposals.

Index: In your blog, you said privacy was 'the new black' for censorship. I thought that was a great way of putting it. Although it might make it appealing in a way you probably didn't intend.

Peter Fleischer: Well, if you take that phrase out of context it sounds very provocative, of course, but the point that I'm trying to make is that historically in democratic countries, in order to implement censorship in the usual sense of the word – to delete someone else's content – you generally had to prove that the speech was untrue. I mean, that was the nature of filing a libel case, or filing a defamation case. And if you won that case then you could essentially censor someone else's content. But privacy doesn't require the content to be untrue, you just claim, 'This is personal information about me. You may not publish it without my consent.'

In the past, the UK in particular was always accused of being a destination for libel tourism. And one of the questions is now, will countries – I'm not pointing the finger at the UK in particular – but will they then become destinations of, let's call it 'privacy litigation tourism', where people say: 'I want to exercise censorship about what you said about me, because it invades my privacy'? And you no longer have to say the speech was untrue – it just invades my privacy. And we see many examples of that cropping up.

The cases in Spain are just a series of examples, but I get examples almost every day – I'm not going to get into specifics – where the data protection authority from somewhere around Europe reaches out to me and asks me or, sometimes, purports to order me, to delete third party content from our platforms. I'm not talking about Google content, these are Google platforms – could be YouTube, could be Blogger, could be others, where users place speech up that someone claims invades their privacy and again they're not claiming the speech is untrue. And that is becoming a very common order, and I think we need a very clear understanding about two things: first, is it the obligation of the platform to make this decision? If it is, then it's Google that's making a censorship decision or not. Obviously we would prefer not to have that responsibility, and we think most people don't want us to have that responsibility. The second question then, is privacy a right that trumps someone else's freedom of expression? That is a very specific policy question that needs to be asked. We do not want to make that decision as an intermediary, as a platform, but someone is going to make that decision and that is the difficult policy question that I think goes to the heart of the conundrum of the right to be forgotten.

Index: Also, in a broader sense in terms of press freedom in the UK, possible conflicts between privacy and freedom of speech have recently become a very big issue since the European Convention on Human Rights became a part of English law. What you are saying about who has responsibility is something that we are actively looking at in terms of libel reform in this country – is it the author or the platform who has liability? It is one of the big challenges for freedom of speech.

Peter Fleischer: Yes. I mean, I am many years into a personal Italian legal saga and so I have personal experience.

Index: What is the status of that?

Peter Fleischer: Well, after my conviction we filed a note of appeal and we expect the appeal process to begin in the fall. So it will have been from conviction to the beginning of the appeal process roughly a year and a half for it to even begin. But we don't know for sure. Time lines keep changing.

It is, of course, relevant to the conversation we are having here because it is a case where three officers of Google – chief legal officer, chief financial officer and myself – were held personally, criminally liable and sentenced to six months in jail for content – a three-minute video – that was taken by some Italian teenagers while they were bullying one of their classmates and put out on the video-sharing platform owned by Google. You know we had nothing to do with the video at all and did not know about it until after the case had been launched. Google took the video down within two hours of receiving notice of it. Nonetheless, three of us were convicted of violating the privacy of the boy who was captured in the video being bullied, so this is a clear example of the intermediary – meaning the video-sharing platform – being held responsible for content that was uploaded by somebody, and in this context for content that was deemed to violate the privacy of the person captured in the video.

So it wasn't untrue content – it was not defamation, it was not libel – it was content that was deemed to violate this person's privacy. A defamation claim had been brought by the prosecutor but was dismissed. The intermediary was held liable for this notwithstanding the e-commerce directive that says intermediaries are not liable for the content that is uploaded on their platforms until they have notice. And it was not only Google that was convicted, it was three individuals at Google. That is the case that is going to appeal in Italy but it is a striking example of a privacy lawsuit and the principles of who is responsible for someone else's speech. And it is fairly obvious that we believe that the e-commerce laws are right – the ones that were passed in Europe a decade ago that say the intermediary platform can't be responsible for the speech until it receives notice thereof and then has an obligation to take it down if the content is bad. So you can see these are issues that are not philosophical and abstract for me – they are also very personal.

Index: I want to move onto another sort of question – a privacy question – which is around the protection of users and specifically users of Gmail. This has been a big issue over the past year for two reasons. First, in terms of what happened in China and Google's decision to pull out after its Gmail users were targeted, among other considerations. And second, the court order that was served on Twitter and the ongoing appeal against this court order.

So there is this big question around how does a company like Google protect its users, particularly when it comes to vulnerable users such as human rights activists perhaps, or journalists in a country like China? What kind of safeguards can there be or what better laws? Obviously one answer is exactly what Google did in China, which was a very bold move. Is there also an argument for pushing for new laws in America?

Peter Fleischer: What we do or did in China is very different than what we would be advocating for in Europe and the US. So, to take those separately, first let's make clear we did not pull out of China. What we said is that we would no longer censor search results in China. So we redirected search queries from China to our uncensored Hong Kong search engine domain. I just wanted to be clear on that because sometimes in the media it was phrased as 'Google pulls out of China'. It was still a dramatic move, don't get me wrong, but I just wanted to be clear on that.

Take Europe and the US separately. In the US there is a law which is over 20 years old that's called the Electronic Communications Privacy Act, and that governs how, when, under what circumstances, governments can order companies like Google to hand over communications like emails. And we have been very active, together with other industry partners, in trying to push Congress to update the Electronic Communications Privacy Act, because it was a law that was passed before the internet. So for example, they have some very different legal standards for content that is over six months old, and it doesn't really make any sense in the context of email services, where you can just delete all archives and your inboxes if you want to. So we have been very active in trying to get that updated and I think we are starting to see traction on that.

In Europe, the debate is really more acute in the context of gathering and retention. There is a European directive which will force all the European countries to pass laws that say that communications service providers must retain data in communication logs, if you will, of all communications – phone calls, emails and so on – for time periods of between six months and 24 months that will vary from country to country. And it's fascinating to me that the rules are not harmonised, so you don't really know what all these conflicting rules are supposed to mean in the real world. And also there have been constitutional challenges and courts could rule that these laws are unconstitutional now in a whole series of countries. The German constitutional court, the Czech constitutional court, the Romanian constitutional court have all ruled that data retention is unconstitutional in their respective countries.

And so the courts are saying, OK, is this invasion of privacy justified? That is the decision that the courts have to make and we have already had three supreme courts in Europe that have decided no. So it is yet another really good example about where privacy is in conflict with other goals – in this context, law enforcement. And you can see how people reach different conclusions, in this case the courts reaching different conclusions about laws being passed in their own countries. We, of course, as just one company in this space are downhill from all of this and we are supposed to comply, but what we are supposed to comply with is very unclear, and varies from country to country.

Peter Fleischer was talking to Jo Glanville

40(2): 78/89
DOI: 10.1177/0306422011409493
www.indexoncensorship.org

Peter Fleischer is Google's global privacy counsel. He has more than ten years' experience in the field of data protection, including his previous position as Microsoft's privacy lead for Europe and director of regulatory affairs.

3
SUPER FICIAL

2
SUPERWOMAN

4
SUPERCILIOUS

6
SUPERFLUOUS

AGE OF INSECURITY

We may have lost the first battle to protect our data, say **Gus Hosein** and **Eric King**, but there's a chance to put things right if we're ready to have the debate

Privacy advocates are often labelled luddites. Don't like a new service created by the coolest and latest billionaire geek-genius-led company? It's because you are a luddite. Don't like the government's latest technology for a new infrastructure of surveillance? Luddite. It's as though we are afraid of technology. It's because we understand these technologies better than most, that many of us became advocates in the first place. We need to know more about technology than the techno-fans. We need to know more than ministers promoting technological solutions to social problems (not hard to do); we need to know as much about security as the security services; we need to know more about communications techniques than the media, and we need to know more about networking than social-networking gurus. This knowledge can be a terrible thing, because everywhere we look we see vulnerabilities. The sad truth is that the entire edifice of modern communications is built upon fragile foundations.

It didn't have to be this way. Privacy advocates lost the argument by allowing governments and industry to define the needs of citizens and users. We would call on companies to strengthen the technical protections in their systems and they would claim that users don't care about security or are uninterested, citing 18-year-olds who want to publicise their private lives or housewives who don't want to be bothered with complex technology. We are now facing tangible and hitherto inconceivable threats to our liberty because the entire edifice of modern communications and information technologies is built upon consumer stereotypes.

It is our collective fault now that there is a rapidly growing number of data breaches and data losses. The systems that were built to contain and protect our information are fundamentally flawed. The flow of personal data is becoming the default, and the dams erected by law are temporary annoyances for an industry interested in profiting, governments interested in monitoring and malicious parties whose motivation can be obscure. If the US State Department can't be bothered to adequately secure its own network of inter-embassy communications, what chance is there that Facebook and Google will take better care of your personal messaging and commonly used search terms?

The irony is that the only debate we privacy advocates ever seriously won was over the right of individuals to use encryption technologies to secure their communications. We fought this battle in the 1990s, on the cusp of the information revolution, looking forward to the day when we would all have desktop computers, and everyone would use encryption technologies to secure their communications. Governments were keen to maintain their restrictions on the general public's ability to encrypt communications so that law enforcement agencies retained unfettered access to content. We fought these restrictions and, even to our surprise, by the end of the decade we eventually won. By this time, however, governments had successfully stemmed the tide: cryptography and other privacy-enhancing technologies had come to be seen as obscure and inconvenient. Everyone is now theoretically capable of encrypting their communications – but no one does. Furthermore, restrictions on encryption remain in countries such as China, India and across the Middle East.

This is indicative of how the entire infrastructure of the modern economy and social life is built on insecurity. Privacy is becoming a popular subject, and a growing concern for the average citizen and consumer of mainstream technology. Yet users' interest is poorly serviced.

This is why there is a frequent narrative that 'privacy is dead'. Regardless of modern concerns, faulty decisions have been made at key moments in the development of modern computing. Microsoft was the first culprit to emphasise ease of use over security in the 1990s, leading to a decade of annoying trojans and viruses developed by teenagers. In response, a software industry of anti-virus checkers and firewalls arose to plug in the holes

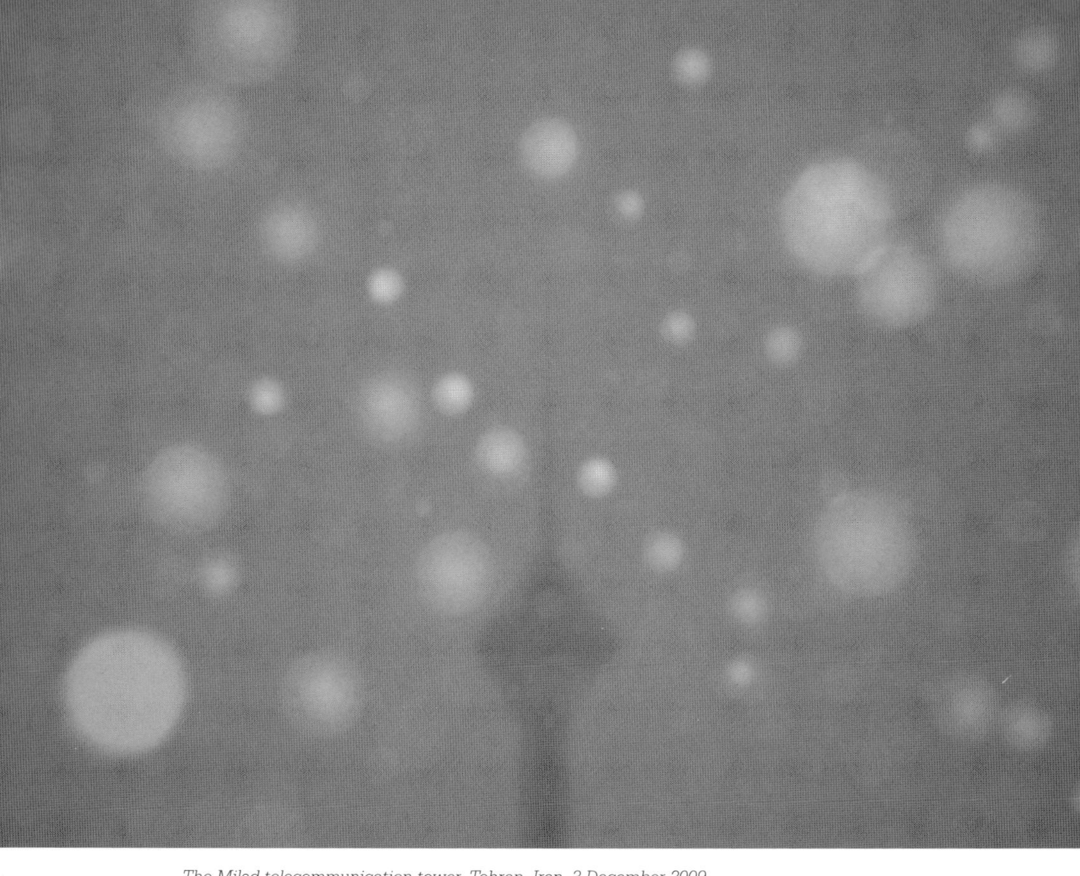

The Milad telecommunication tower, Tehran, Iran, 3 December 2009
Credit: Morteza Nikoubazl/Reuters

so that users were informed and protected from attack. We had the chance to learn from this and make our next technological steps more informed and considered. Instead, Smartphone operating system developers like Apple and Google are now making similar mistakes by not keeping their users informed of what kind of information is leaving their devices and what applications are doing with their data. This is a repetition of Facebook's approach when they created features that broadly shared users' information, only later adding some features to inform users and to let them have some authority to control information flows when using third-party applications. Once your information is collected by devices and applications, as we have seen from Microsoft in the 1990s, and now Apple, Google and Facebook, it is rarely secure. In fact, your data is often readily available to any party who can query, buy, subpoena or simply steal it.

The expansion of 'cloud' services like Google Documents or Dropbox makes matters even worse. Instead of residing on your computers, your most confidential information is not only removed from your control, it is removed from the country and stored on foreign servers under the jurisdiction of foreign laws and law enforcement agencies. Almost universally, this information is not secured. Documents, emails and calendar information are stored in unencrypted form, and readily accessible by local law enforcement authorities.

Amongst the few positive developments, Google recently deployed disk encryption capabilities in its mobile operating system, Android, though it still has to be turned on by the user. Even when these companies do build in the capabilities for privacy, they rarely, if ever, come as standard. Security is the exception rather than the rule. After the Russian authorities began clamping down on Russian non-governmental organisations for breach of copyright (as a pretence for searching computers), Microsoft then kindly offered free versions of its operating systems to NGOs. Unfortunately, the version of Windows they offered does not include the use of disk encryption, as that is only available in the 'premium' editions.

At the core of this problem is companies' perception of their typical user. The typical user in whose image applications, programs and social networks are designed is an American teenager, perfectly content to transmit and publish every detail of their personal life to an unlimited audience. It is not the advocate, the dissident, the researcher, the professional – the people who need varying degrees of data security in order to protect their livelihoods, and sometimes their lives. Facebook, Apple, Microsoft and Google all require their users to jump through hoops in order to protect their information, and the majority of these users lack the time or awareness to do so.

In turn, companies' systems are being probed, and vulnerabilities are being exploited. Last year, a gang in New Hampshire used 'publicly available' social network updates from area residents to target addresses when they knew the homeowners were out or away, stealing over US$100,000 worth of property in a week. A survey of hackers and security experts last year found that more than half of them were testing the limits of cloud services' security. Meanwhile, last year a Google employee was fired after it was discovered that he was monitoring the communications of teenage girls.

Far more widespread, insidious and difficult to combat than such isolated incidents of criminality are the routine surveillance practices conducted by governments. These are not techniques reserved for dictatorships. For instance, the spying capabilities embedded by Nokia Siemens in their technology for Iran's telecommunications system, intended for the use of the Iranian authorities, were mandated by the Clinton administration under federal law applying to all US telecommunications firms, and then supported

HOW TO USE FACEBOOK (SAFELY)

Activism is defined not just by a belief in the need for change, the right to inspire change and the strength of purpose to initiate action, but also by the tools available to fully empower that commitment. Facebook, and other forms of social networking, have established their value to advocacy by enabling activists to reach further than ever before and mobilise a critical mass.

We spent months researching how vulnerable people protect themselves, studying the needs of the world's more exposed people, from activists to society's outcasts. We tried all the settings, reviewed all the studies. We badly wanted to come up with the ultimate guide.

So what can you do if you are gay in Uganda, or an abused spouse living in seclusion in England and don't want this information disclosed? What can you do if you are a journalist in China or a whistleblower in the US? How can you engage with Facebook's world without causing harm, information leakage, relationship disclosures, and affiliations? And how can you trust Facebook?

Here is a guide on how best to keep using Facebook and stay safe.

Use a fake name: Facebook is adamant that you must use your real name, as printed on your national ID card. Of course you can set up a pseudonymous account for your 'activist account' with a secondary email address, but the process itself isn't anonymous and you may be outed through network analysis. That is, you can be identified by the company you keep. And you can be traced back to your computer if the authorities ask Facebook for identifying information (after they boot you off for using a fake name). In this case, using circumvention tools like Tor to anonymise your internet traffic will help prevent you from being traced.

Confuse your profile: You can confuse people by joining contradictory groups ('Lovers of Falun Gong' and 'Haters of Falun Gong') so that anyone who is trying to categorise you will be confused. But even a simple form of analysis will identify those with confused identities. Remember, too, that adversaries have been known to create fake profiles and fake events. It's important to do all you can to validate authenticity, and to do so repeatedly, as accounts of previously validated friends may be subsequently compromised.

Don't trust privacy settings: There is almost universal confusion over what Facebook deems 'publicly available information', and in view of the social network's enthusiasm to change its policies, you can never rest assured that these settings are strong. To compound this problem, applications could open up your social graph. As well as using the strongest privacy settings, enabling HTTPS on your Facebook account security page is vital to help defend against interception, whether it is by a malicious wifi network in a cafe or a malicious government monitoring data flows in and out of the country. While HTTPS does not provide perfect security, it is usually a critically significant defensive measure even when it isn't totally impregnable.

Log in, log off: Did you know that once you have logged into Facebook and closed your browser tab but not logged back out, Facebook will be notified of every related site you visit where it runs services? Unless you are careful enough to log off on every occasion, you are susceptible to tracking. Facebook will have a log of you on any news organisation site where articles have a 'like' button.

Does any of this matter? You could reason that Facebook does employ responsible and caring people, after all. We know many Facebook employees and we regard them highly. This is beside the point. Facebook is required to respond to government requests for user information. How will it respond to requests from law enforcement agencies around the world? The fact of the matter is that we do not know. While Facebook remains outside the Global Network Initiative whose mandate is to help technology companies protect freedom of expression and privacy, then we cannot be certain if they will contest requests from foreign law enforcement agencies.

Simon Davies is the director of Privacy International

Eric King is the human rights and technology advisor at Privacy International and technology advisor at Reprieve by European policy-makers and standards bodies under the more acceptable guise (or pretence) of protecting their own citizens from crime.

Some countries, like Sweden, openly acknowledge that every piece of information that enters or leaves their borders is subject to government surveillance. Whether you're a journalist sworn to protect the names and addresses of your sources, a lawyer building a case against a corrupt high-profile politician, or a human rights advocate, all are pinning their hopes for security on a fantasy: the belief that the people who build your operating systems and applications have any way (or, indeed, any intention) of protecting you against governments who have the law on their side.

Another part of the fantasy is that governments are in control. Disturbingly, in fact, they don't even appear to have complete mastery of their spying capabilities; for ten months during 2004–2005, the Greek government's own surveillance technology was turned against it when an unknown adversary monitored the voice calls of dozens of government officials and cabinet members, including the prime minister. Between 1996 and 2006, Telecom Italia had a similar breach where more than 6,000 individuals' communications were illegally monitored, for the purpose of perpetrating blackmail and bribery. As communications security expert Susan Landau noted in her testimony to the US Congress in February this year, in that period 'no large business or political deal was ever truly private'.

Surveillance is getting easier. In the Hollywood version of governmental power, the seizure of digital evidence by the security services involves a dawn raid by armed officials, who carry off piles of hard drives, laptops and computer towers from seemingly innocuous suburban houses. This image is out of date and unrepresentative. In the 21st century, law enforcement access is just a few clicks of the mouse away. Why enter your home and read your letters when they can get into your webmail account and read every message you've ever sent or received? In the US, a member of staff at one of the major mobile providers recently let slip at an intelligence industry conference that the company receives eight million requests a year from domestic law enforcement agencies for specific data on geolocation; that's a publicly traded company, one that advertises its services on billboards and TV channels across the country, not some shadowy private intelligence outfit operating under the radar.

There are companies in the business of surveillance that develop the databases, cameras, biometric scanners, DNA test kits, drones and a myriad other technologies that are being deployed around the world. Companies are also profiting from selling and buying personal information. Consider Thorpe Glenn, an Ipswich-based company that celebrates its ability to

A policeman films activists at a news conference near the US embassy in Seoul, 8 April 2010
Credit: Lee Jae Won/Reuters

analyse the information of 50m mobile subscribers in less than a fortnight. Thorpe Glenn's press releases boast about 'maintaining the world's largest social network', with a full 700m more profiles than even Facebook can lay claim to. This practice is rapidly becoming an industry.

Chris Soghoian, a researcher in the US, has found that companies frequently get paid for each instance they respond to government requests. Google, for example, has received US$25 for responding to a request for data from the US Marshal Service. Yahoo!'s 'Cost Reimbursement Policy' offers US$20 dollars for the first basic subscriber record and then a discounted US$10 per ID thereafter, though email content is US$30–$40 per user. They could, technically, develop a business model just on handing over information to law enforcement agencies. Jokes aside, what incentive do these providers have to make communications infrastructure more secure?

There are, however, some signs of change. Over the past year some companies have announced security and privacy advances in their products and services. Certainly the uprisings across the Arab world helped, as companies did not want to be seen on the wrong side of history and face the same kind of admonishment as Nokia Siemens after the Iranian elections in 2009. Google vacillated for years before turning on encryption on its network layer, but it is swiftly becoming common practice. It is to be hoped that we will see a similar paradigm shift now that Facebook has enabled users to turn on HTTPS to help protect data as it passes through the internet (although predictably enough it has yet to employ HTTPS by default, making it less easy for people to use it). The global struggles against abusive governments have also focused international attention on the enormous capacities of those governments to spy on their citizens, and the enormous human cost of this kind of all-pervasive surveillance. Once the behemoths of the internet take positive steps, smaller companies will hopefully follow.

Yet so long as the key technology developers keep on assuming that their users are uninterested, and so long as they seek to profit by selling our habits and interests, we will all remain vulnerable. It is now time for a mature policy debate on privacy and security. Not one that sees the benefit of the state as paramount, nor one that presumes that if a service is free then the user's information can be exploited. Business models should fail with each security and privacy blunder, just as laws should be called into question with every new breach and abuse. The rise of mobile devices and cloud services is a replay of the 1990s all over again, where the policy and business world is grappling with technological change and telecommunications growth. If left to their own devices, governments will build more vulnerabilities and back doors while industry will acquiesce and build for 'sharing' and 'organising the world's information'. If we can hold on to this moment in history just a bit longer, and keep these companies thinking about the global community of diverse users, and not merely those who are 18 years old, while reminding them that backdoors aren't always used for noble purposes, then we may have a fighting chance. Perhaps we can even chalk up a real win this time. ❐

40(2): 92/100
DOI: 10.1177/0306422011410787
www.indexoncensorship.org

Gus Hosein is deputy director of Privacy International. He is also a visiting senior fellow at the London School of Economics and Political Science.

Eric King is the Human Rights and Technology Advisor at Privacy International and Technology Advisor at Reprieve.

Miller-McCune
Original research-based
news for policy makers,
academics and the media
fn
solutions
Smart Journalism.
Real Solutions.
Find the latest on policy,
business, media, culture and
the environment at
Miller-McCune.com

FRIENDS, USERS, CITIZENS

When the US government came for Icelandic MP **Birgitta Jónsdóttir**'s private information, she grew concerned about the lack of protection for rights online

Last December, the US Department of Justice served a court order on Twitter, seeking private information about me, Jacob Appelbaum and Ron Gonggrijp. We had all worked with WikiLeaks and the order appeared to be part of the US's comprehensive information sweep in the fallout from the publication of the diplomatic cables last year. The court order was sealed – which meant that none of us could be informed about the request. Had it not been for Twitter's decision to challenge the government's demand for secrecy, no one would ever have known about it. In March, following a legal battle, a Virginia court ruled that the government was allowed to collect our private records from Twitter. The court also decided that we could not find out which other internet companies had been ordered to turn over information about us to the government. The judgment is being appealed.

As a result of this experience, I have become increasingly worried about social media users' lack of rights. Before my Twitter case, I didn't think much about what I might be risking when signing up to user agreements with online companies. The text is usually lengthy and written in a legal language that most people don't understand, so

Protest supporting WikiLeaks founder Julian Assange outside Westminster Magistrates Court, London, 14 December 2010
Credit: Karel Prinsloo/AP/Press

I think it is safe to say that nearly all of us who click that button do so in a blind faith that the legalities of the internet won't apply in the real world.

What I have learned about my lack of rights in the last few months demonstrates that there is a need to raise awareness and improve the quality of legal guidelines. Many of us who use the internet – whether to write emails, browse its growing landscape, mine for information, connect with others or organise ourselves – are not aware that our behaviour is being monitored. Online profiling has become a default with companies such as Google and Facebook: huge databases record our every move within their landscape in order to direct advertising at us. In their world, we have so far not been fully regarded as citizens with civil rights to defend, but as a commodity. This notion needs to change. To be fair, no one really knew where we were heading in the beginning. Neither we, the users, nor the companies gathering and storing our personal information for profit. Very few of us had the imagination to predict that governments that claim to be democratic would invade our online privacy with no regard to our rights in the real world. We might look to China and other totalitarian states and expect them to violate the free flow of information and human rights online, but not our own democratic governments.

I guess the dilemma we are facing is that there is no proper standard nor basic laws in place that deal with the fundamental question: are we to be treated as consumers or citizens online? There is no international charter that says we should have the same rights as citizens in the real world. Our legal systems are slow compared to the speed of development online. With the social media explosion many people have put very sensitive information about themselves and others into databases without knowing that they have few rights to defend themselves against attempts by governments to obtain their personal data.

According to the ruling of the judge in the Twitter case, we forfeit those rights when we agree to the terms and conditions of the company hosting our data, if it is kept on servers in the US. We have to rely on companies such as Amazon, Facebook, Google or Twitter to look out for us, when it might not always be in their business interests to protect us. I want to stress that Twitter did fight for the interests of its users by going to court to unseal the court order, which demanded that they hand over personal user information within three days. If Twitter had not been successful, we would never have discovered the extent of the Department of Justice's demand for our data in the borderless legal jungle. I am, for example, not an American citizen and am therefore not protected by the First and Fourth Amendments in the US constitution.

The reason we make international treaties and declarations about human rights is because somewhere along the line we have agreed that certain rights are sacred and universal. We need to make the same principles apply to our human rights online, as well as offline. These two worlds have fused together and it is no longer possible to define them as distinct any more.

Many of us now have a significant history online, which has to be protected by the same privacy regulations that apply when someone attempts to enter our homes uninvited or obtain permission to tap our phones. I would also like to know why the US authorities are so intent on criminalising WikiLeaks that they found it necessary to seek, in secret, the private information of a member of parliament of a sovereign nation. Will the US in future be able to protect its own politicians from similar privacy violations abroad? Members of parliament all over the world are encouraged to use social media to be in touch with their voters. Many voters might send sensitive information about themselves to their MPs or senators online, without realising that sending a message on Facebook or via Twitter or Gmail is not an official pathway.

The same principles apply online as well as offline

Since the Virginia court ruled in favour of exposing private information about me, a foreign politician, there are urgent questions about the privacy and sovereignty of individuals in cyberspace that need to be addressed. There has to be a debate on both a global and local scale on what should remain secret or sacred and what kind of information should not be put into public or even private circulation. There needs to be education and clarification on users' rights. Some social media companies guard their users – while others don't – and legal guidelines are essential. Until then, all we can do is trust in the social media companies to watch our backs.

And here's a tip to authorities who don't want to let go of their big brother tendencies: it is a lot easier for the cybercitizen to migrate in cyberspace than it is in the real world. People don't like to have their privacy invaded for no good reason: if their rights are not respected, there could be a massive exodus of information refugees from US-hosted companies to countries that are less hostile. ❒

For further information, go to the Electronic Frontier Foundation campaign 'When the government comes knocking who has your back?': https://www.eff.org/pages/when-government-comes-knocking-who-has-your-back.

40(2): 102/106
DOI: 10.1177/0306422011411536
www.indexoncensorship.org

Birgitta Jónsdóttir is a member of the Icelandic parliament. She is also a writer, artist and activist. She was a volunteer for WikiLeaks and campaigned to make Iceland a haven for press freedom.

A man dressed as a surveillance camera at a demonstration against state and corporate surveillance, Berlin, September 2009
Credit: Thomas Peter/Reuters

WEB SPIES

Does it matter that companies are collecting data? More than you might imagine, warns **Paul Bernal**

A couple of years ago I suggested at a conference, very tentatively, the idea of a system that would alert users with a little light every time someone started watching their activities online. The idea was almost laughed at: so many different organisations, companies and people watch us that our screens would light up like a Christmas tree. We are watched, and data is gathered about us, on such a regular basis that to monitor those who are tracking us is already a mammoth task.

The majority of those watching, tracking and profiling us are doing so for commercial purposes. Google, for example, records everything we search for, as well as which links we follow, primarily so that it can sharpen its service – but also so that it can target its advertising more precisely. It doesn't require a conspiracy theory to understand why it does so – it's all about finding ways to make more money.

That kind of monitoring, however, is just a small part of the picture. The entertainment industry is always looking at new ways to monitor those who might be downloading music and movies in breach of copyright. There are other motives too: in 2005 the developers of the hugely successful online game World of Warcraft added a little piece of software to monitor their users' activities – every website visited, every piece of software launched, every window opened – to check whether those playing the game were trying to cheat. Even non-commercial web providers, such as the BBC, monitor what we do – to find out which parts of their sites are being used and which links are being followed – so that they can sharpen their websites, making them more attractive and better to use.

Entire industries are also developing around being able to divine all kinds of the most intimate and personal information about anyone who surfs the internet. The monitoring of users' behaviour online is becoming increasingly sophisticated to target advertising. This kind of information can be highly sensitive and, in the hands of the wrong people, highly damaging.

A prime example of this is Phorm, a company that became very controversial in the UK in 2009 – and whose story raises both alarm and hope. Alarm because of what it tried to do – and hope because it failed, and more importantly because of the way in which it failed. Its system, known as Webwise, works through ISPs to monitor a user's web-browsing activity, using the information to categorise, profile them and allow the instant targeting of advertising. This monitoring is achieved through the use of a little technical subterfuge. When a user tries to access any website, an instruction is sent to the server where the website is hosted, asking for the page requested. Phorm's Webwise intercepts all those instructions, records them and sends a 'cookie'(a little computer file that maintains a record of the user's activities and preferences for using a particular website) to the user's computer. The Phorm cookie masquerades as a cookie sent by the website the user intended to visit. That cookie then records, and delivers to Phorm, all the user's activities on the website; combined with all the other Phorm cookies, a profile of the user's entire web-browsing activities is created that can be used to target advertising.

Phorm signed deals with BT, TalkTalk and Virgin Media in 2008, and there was an outcry when BT admitted that it had been conducting trials without users' consent. Nicholas Bohm, general counsel for the Foundation for Information Policy Research (FIPR), claimed that any ISP deploying Phorm would not only be in breach of data protection law through the way the system gathered personal data, but also the Regulation of Investigatory Powers Act (RIPA) through intercepting instructions to web-servers. Bohm further judged that any ISP using Phorm would be guilty of fraud.

Even so, Phorm had managed to get extensive support, first from the ISPs – who saw a potentially lucrative source of advertising income – and then from the UK government, for reasons that were never entirely clear, but were probably connected to the idea of encouraging innovative business ideas. Leaked emails, in April 2009, also pointed to a possible collusion between the Home Office and Phorm to find a way to suggest that the company was not in breach of either RIPA or the Data Protection Act – something that the then Liberal Democrat home affairs spokeswoman, Baroness Sue Miller, called 'jaw-dropping' and 'bizarre'.

The government's support for this invasion of personal privacy was deeply disturbing to many; a furore followed, effectively marshalled by advocacy groups such as the Open Rights Group. Questions were asked in Parliament and legal action was threatened, particularly over the secret trials in which more than 30,000 BT internet customers had their web browsing monitored without either their knowledge or any semblance of consent. Eventually this even led to legal action by the European Commission, also in 2009, suggesting that if the UK thought this kind of activity complied with data protection and privacy law then it cannot have implemented the relevant European directives appropriately. As a result of this, Phorm's commercial partners abandoned it and the company had to give up trying to launch Webwise in the UK. In April, the Crown Prosecution Service announced that it would not be prosecuting either BT or Phorm for alleged interception of browsing data.

The defeat of Phorm, despite support from both business and government, is a very positive sign. Also positive are two initiatives, from both sides of the Atlantic. In Europe, the highly controversial Cookies Directive came into force in May. This directive – actually a modification of existing directives – seems to require prior and explicit consent for the installation or use of any cookie on any computer. There is a lot of doubt as to how it will work in practice and the advertising industry is up in arms, lobbying hard that it is unnecessary, impractical and impossible to implement. It also claims that the directive can be complied with by doing little more than changing browser settings. In the US, meanwhile, the Do Not Track initiative (DNT), working through apparent co-operation between advertisers and the makers of browsing software – Microsoft, Google and Mozilla – has gained momentum and the latest versions of all these browsers include ways to implement the scheme. The idea behind DNT is that it will work like the 'do not call' systems, where people can opt not to receive cold calls from advertisers. The Obama administration has even suggested a 'privacy bill of rights' for the internet, which would provide legal backing for the DNT initiative. This proposal was first put to Congress in March and focuses on the advertising industry.

None of these initiatives, however, is likely to be particularly effective. The Cookies Directive and the DNT initiatives are far too specific, designed to deal with one particular form of technology – the cookie – while those who really want to monitor and track people actually have a much wider set of options. 'Flash cookies', which use a different and more sophisticated technology to do much the same thing – but can also 're-spawn' previously deleted cookies – is one possibility. What is misleadingly called 'browser fingerprinting' is another. This relies on the settings information that your web-browsing software sends to a website – such as which version of the software you're using and what kind of computer you're using – so that the page is sent back to you in an appropriate form. Research by the Electronic Frontier Foundation has shown that this kind of information can identify individuals more than 90 per cent of the time.

Even more importantly, none of these initiatives really addresses the underlying issues, in part at least because the problem isn't understood broadly enough: in all cases they work on the assumption that this is only really about advertising, and hence just an inconvenience or an annoyance, but not really any kind of threat. However, the data that is gathered about us – particularly when it is done covertly – can be used for many purposes. What is more, the data gatherers know this, so hold on to that data and look for ways to make money from it, for example by selling it to other parties, mostly for marketing purposes. Secondly, the whole idea of monitoring and profiling people's internet use has become such a lucrative area that the boundaries are being pushed all the time, both technically and ethically –as the cautionary tale of Phorm illustrates.

Information gathered commercially may be accessed or used by governments. Data retention, as set out in the European Data Retention Directive, is one of the key areas in which this is happening. Providers of communications services – from landline and mobile phone operators to providers of email services and indeed internet service providers – are required to gather and hold traffic data about all communications and make it available to appropriate authorities for the investigation of 'serious crime' (what constitutes 'serious crime' may vary between member states; benefit fraud, for example, might constitute serious crime in the UK). This data, which records who you talk to and send or receive messages to and from – though not the content of the messages – must be held for a period of at least six months, the period dependent on the particular member state's implementation. Peter Hustinx, the European data protection supervisor, has called it 'the most privacy-invasive piece of legislation ever adopted by the European Union'. It covers pretty much every type of electronic communication.

Other means of gathering our data are also regularly employed. The US government has at different times served court orders and subpoenas on both Google and Twitter for access to user information. The Chinese authorities have in the past had the co-operation of Yahoo! in locating and eventually imprisoning dissidents. Even more critically, it is hard to know how often other commercial organisations have simply complied with requests from various authorities for information: cases only become public knowledge when those holding the data show resistance. Businesses are not often willing to go against government wishes: consider the alacrity with which Amazon, PayPal, Visa Europe and MasterCard quickly fell in with the US government's desire to punish WikiLeaks.

Some governments also appear not to be averse to using illegal tactics. The former Tunisian government hacked into Facebook's log-in page, altering it so that when anyone in Tunisia logged in, their user name and password were automatically sent to the authorities, who could then access their account and find out what they were doing, who they were talking to and what they were organising. This case – and the way that the Egyptian authorities effectively 'switched off' the internet – brought protests from

The US Justice Department ordered Twitter to release the private information of several of its users, including that of Icelandic MP Birgitta Jónsdóttir, in January 2011
Credit: AP Photo/HO

many in the West. The US Secretary of State, Hillary Clinton, even gave a key speech about the importance of freedom on the internet, something that privacy advocates thought ironic at best, since at the same time the FBI was suggesting that tech companies should be required to build 'back doors' in their infrastructure to allow for data interception.

Nevertheless, some key commercial organisations are beginning to understand the importance of privacy, and take the side of the individual user. When the US government served a court order on Twitter earlier this year for the personal information of individuals associated with WikiLeaks, it added a 'gagging order', preventing Twitter from disclosing the fact of the order either to the media or to the users concerned. Twitter had the strength to challenge the gagging order in the courts – and win. The court order itself has not been overturned – but the way that Twitter stood up for the rights of its users deserves to be applauded [see pp.102–106].

Google has also been showing signs that it understands the issues – and is beginning to take a more friendly stance towards privacy. In a recent blog, Alma Whitten, Google's director of privacy for product and engineering, explicitly acknowledged the need for its users to employ anonymity and pseudonyms at times. As Twitter and Google begin to come on board, other big internet players need to be encouraged to follow.

Human rights and privacy advocates should bring the issue more clearly into the public domain. When individuals and experts have stood up and protested, businesses have responded. We need to make it much clearer that we do have rights – and that those rights need to be respected by governments and businesses. To do that, we need to make privacy something that is in itself seen as a virtue that will attract customers, business and votes. Appropriate laws are then more likely to make their way onto the statute books and are more likely to be properly enforced.

Our rights also need to be built into the infrastructure of the internet. We need to fight against pernicious developments, such as data retention or compulsory back doors into our email or social networking services, and ensure that the systems developed by businesses allow us the freedom and control that we need – and make the deletion of data possible. We need to find ways to make business work to protect us from snooping rather than help those who want to snoop.

As long as we focus only on governments and don't address the reality of the commercial internet, we will find that rather than being a positive force for human rights, the internet will become more of a tool for oppression and control. Big Brother still wants to watch us, but right now his commercial partners are the ones doing a great deal of the watching.

40(2): 108/114
DOI: 10.1177/0306422011409312
www.indexoncensorship.org

Paul Bernal is a lecturer in information technology, intellectual property and media law at the University of East Anglia and a member of Media@UEA. His research interests include privacy on the internet

THE POLITICS OF SURVEILLANCE

Political opponents and activists are among those monitored in Latin America. **Katitza Rodríguez** charts the erosion of privacy in the region

While most Latin American countries have democratically-elected governments, many still fail to respect human rights, including the right to privacy. Across the region, there have been multiple scandals involving government officials and intelligence agencies engaged in illegal surveillance of communications. These include numerous chilling examples of how interception technologies are being misused to spy on politicians, dissidents, judges, human rights organisations and activists. Although privacy violations vary from country to country, and the full extent of government surveillance in the region remains largely unknown, newly disclosed data gathering programmes hint at the architecture of surveillance lying beneath the surface of ostensibly democratic societies.

These surveillance systems demonstrate how communication interception is being used as a political tool to identify, control and stifle dissent. Their use also highlights the lack of transparency and accountability that surrounds pervasive government surveillance in many Latin American countries. In 2009, Colombia's 'Las Chuzadas' scandal revealed that members of the country's intelligence service allegedly carried out illegal, widespread

Colombia's President Alvaro Uribe announces he's no longer allowing wiretapping by Colombia's domestic intelligence agency, 26 February 2009
Credit: Fernando Vergara/AP

surveillance and wiretapping of key politicians, judges, dissidents and human rights NGOs. Litigation about the surveillance is currently pending in the Colombian courts. In March 2011, the Inter-American Commission on Human Rights opened an investigation into the role of Colombian state officials in executing this mass surveillance programme.

Perhaps the most severe instance of widespread government surveillance took place in Peru during the presidency of Alberto Fujimori. Fujimori, who is currently in jail, was convicted of mass illegal surveillance of prominent Peruvian citizens. Peruvian prosecutors found that the former president devised and implemented 'Plan Emilio' to conduct nationwide surveillance of politicians, ministers, journalists and activists. In 2010, judicial authorities in Peru discovered a former naval intelligence employee illegally intercepted 52,947 emails from journalists and political opponents of the Fujimori government between 1999 and 2000. The case has yet to go to court.

Leaked US diplomatic cables posted on the WikiLeaks whistleblower website shed light on the US Drug Enforcement Administration's (DEA) communications surveillance programme and how the governments of Paraguay and Panama pressured the US government to allow the use of these technologies for operations unrelated to narcotics investigations. According to the cables, both countries sought US cooperation to expand their respective capacities to spy on mobile communications for political gain.

In Paraguay, this surveillance was undertaken ostensibly to deal with the threat of the leftist guerrilla group the Paraguayan People's Army. A diplomatic cable dated 18 February 2010 reveals that the DEA conducted an active mobile phone spying programme for counter-narcotics efforts in Paraguay beginning in 2009. The cables also reveal that the Paraguayan government requested access to the software used by the DEA to perform eavesdropping for other purposes. US diplomats even warned about the possibility that these surveillance technologies could be misused for unrestricted eavesdropping and political advantage:

> The ambassador made clear that the US had no interest in involving itself in the intercept programme if the potential existed for it to be abused for political gain, but confirmed US interest in cooperating on an intercept programme with safeguards, as long as it included counter-narcotics. While noting that the Interior Ministry's current personnel are trustworthy, the ambassador noted that others could abuse this technology in the future.

The US embassy repeatedly denied Paraguayan government requests for unrestricted access to its surveillance software. According to the US envoy, the interior minister of Paraguay disclosed that his government's 'top priority was capturing the [Paraguayan People's Army], which had to take precedence over counter-narcotics'. 'Counter-narcotics are important,' he said, 'but won't topple our government. The [Paraguayan People's Army] could.'

The cables also reveal the nature of 'cooperation' between US law enforcement and Paraguayan telecom companies, illustrating how the US influenced otherwise hesitant actors:

> TIGO (Millicom), one of Paraguay's leading cell phone providers, told the Ambassador that though they had concerns about the [Government of Paraguay's] decision to move forward with

an intercept programme, they felt that US involvement in the programme would provide them with some 'cover'.

Despite their misgivings, US embassy staff concluded that they could not refuse to cooperate indefinitely without threatening the DEA's broader agenda. 'Get on board or get left behind,' reads the sub-title of the cable. 'If we are not supportive,' the cable continues, 'the [Government of Paraguay] will view us as an obstacle to a key priority, which could jeopardise our broader relationship and the DEA's ability to pursue counter-narcotics leads ... We have carefully navigated this very sensitive and politically sticky situation, and hope that we can move forward quickly in order to make the most of it.' In effect, the US government acknowledged its surveillance assistance would likely be misused for political surveillance, but continued to cooperate.

A similar dynamic played out in Panama. According to a leaked cable dated 22 August 2009, 'Panama 000639', the Panamanian government, headed by President Ricardo Martinelli, repeatedly requested technical assistance from the US to extend its wiretapping capacity. In July 2009, Martinelli sent a BlackBerry message to the ambassador that read, 'I need help with tapping phones.' Moreover, Martinelli sought the DEA's cooperation to acquire US government support for his politically-driven wiretap project. As embassy staff report in the cables, Martinelli thought it was unfair that the 'DEA collects information but that Panama does not benefit from that information'. In his communication with the embassy, he made reference to various groups and individuals he thought should be wiretapped and 'he clearly made no distinction between legitimate security targets and political enemies'. Martinelli went on to say that the US government 'should give the [Government of Panama] its own independent wiretap capability as "rent" in exchange for the use of [its] facilities'.

When the Panamanian government threatened to reduce its cooperation with the counter-narcotics surveillance programme, the US ambassador to Panama counter-threatened to inform his superiors in Washington DC: 'The ambassador forcefully defended the DEA program and pointed out that the jointly-investigated cases were taking criminals off of Panama's streets and making the country safer. ... She would readily inform Washington [of his threat] and [everyone would see] Panama's reputation as a reliable partner plummet dramatically.'

Although Martinelli backed off, the Panamanian government subsequently confirmed that it could expand the wiretapping programme on its own, and had already met with the heads of Panama's four mobile phone operators to discuss methods for obtaining mobile call data. The US

Police outside the National Intelligence Service headquarters in Lima following the release of information about the government's illegal surveillance programme, 18 September 2000
Credit: Pilar Olivares/Reuters

ambassador encouraged the Panamanian government to 'streamline' its process for obtaining emergency court orders for lawful interception, but expressed concerns in another cable about political pressure undermining the independence of the judiciary. According to the cables, Martinelli 'chided' the ambassador's advice for being 'too legal'.

US government officials defended their own wiretap programme in the cables, stating, '[it] works well and upholds the rule of law [and] would easily withstand public scrutiny were it to come to light'. In its coordination with Panamanian authorities to meet US government collection requirements, officials cautioned 'against the danger of local officials trying to commandeer the program for internal political games' and attempted to 'only conduct limited law enforcement wiretap programs in cooperation with Panamanian law enforcement and judicial authorities, directed only against genuine law enforcement targets, in a process managed by a Panamanian prosecutor and approved by a Panamanian Supreme Court judge'. The effectiveness of legal safeguards against interception of communications depends on government compliance with national law. This disclosure shows why we cannot assume that governments will always comply.

Another cable, dated 24 December 2009, reveals that the US decision to remove the DEA's Matador wiretap programme from Panamanian government control was met with resistance and more threats, citing 'a series of obstacles, including threats from the Council for Public Security and National Defense director to expel the DEA from Panama and restrict payments to vetted units and generally weak support for the move from Martinelli and senior [government] leaders'. The US ambassador added that the embassy remained concerned about ongoing efforts by the Panamanian government to weaken judicial controls over domestic surveillance and undermine civil liberties at a time when Panama's judicial institutions were under assault by the executive branch.

'With Panama's notoriously corrupt judicial system (rated 103 out of 133 by the World Economic Forum),' it stated, 'We are not confident that the new judge will uphold the same standards and civil liberties protections that the Panama supreme court has exercised in its oversight of Matador to date.' The ambassador warned his colleagues that the DEA surveillance system should not be used to compromise democratic values in the name of security.

The ambassador concluded by urging the US government not to get entangled in politically motivated wiretapping, advising against involvement in 'questionable activities' in Panama. 'The recent [Las Chuzadas] scandal in Colombia illustrates the catastrophic consequences of politically motivated wiretaps,' he wrote, 'and such a scenario could easily unfold in Panama if the government of Paraguay continues its present course of action. If we cannot guarantee with a high level of confidence that the Matador program will not be misused for political purposes, then we prefer to suspend the program.' Clearly, the ambassador understood the potential dangers posed by the misuse of DEA surveillance systems and how they could be used to undermine free expression and other democratic principles promoted by US policy.

State surveillance can also be achieved through real name registration requirements for the purchase of a mobile phone or SIM card activation. In several countries, there is an emerging trend towards eliminating anonymous communication. Peru, Brazil and Mexico have adopted regulations that compel telecommunications companies to collect and identify pre-paid mobile users' contact information for later potential use by law enforcement entities. A similar bill is being discussed in Guatemala. These measures seek to facilitate the identification of criminals and address the alleged threat to security created by the type of mobile phone account that does not require registration or the collection of detailed personal information.

These registration regimes strike a heavy blow against anonymous communications; citizens not suspected of any crime are denied the use of anonymous pre-paid cell phones to communicate. In some countries like Peru and Brazil, these identification requirements have been extended to cyber cafes, the medium in which a significant proportion of the population with low incomes accesses the internet.

To obtain a mobile phone number in Mexico, citizens are required to provide proof of their current address, present the unique identity code given to both citizens and residents of Mexico, produce valid photo identification, and submit to fingerprint scanning. In accordance with the law, Mexican mobile phone companies are responsible for encouraging the users of their 80m devices to register with the National Registry of Mobile Phone Users. In April 2011, Salvador Guerrero, an authority at the Institute for Access to Public Information of the Federal District, criticised the National Register of Mobile Phone Users for failing to protect the personal data of Mexican citizens: 'During the past year it has become clear that the [registry] is not capable of complying with the function for which it was designed and that is to prevent extortion and kidnapping, the latter figure increasing by eight per cent in 2010 compared to 2009.'

In a few countries, registration requirements are being extended beyond mobiles to internet cafes. In Peru, internet cafes are compelled to register the users of their facilities. Brazil adopted a similar measure in April 2011. The sponsor of the Brazilian legislation, Representative Alex Sandro, said of the measure, 'It will be like the pre-paid phone, which established a registry for the purchase [of pre-paid phones], and the crimes that were committed on these devices still exist, but will decrease greatly because of the possibility of screening.' But this mandate violates the right to speak anonymously, and hinders its crucial function in people's political and social discourse.

People should be able to use the internet anonymously to share sensitive information and express unpopular or controversial opinions without fear of retaliation. The tendency to associate anonymity with criminality by some government officials and law enforcement agencies is troubling. Anonymity is necessary for citizens engaged in legitimate opposition to government policies and for whistleblowers who leak information that those in power would prefer to erase. It is also critical for victims of violence, those who have experienced discrimination because of HIV/Aids, dissidents, homosexuals and survivors of abuse.

Almost all Latin American countries protect the right to privacy in their constitutions, and a number of countries have signed and/or ratified the UN International Covenant on Civil and Political Rights. But many countries have not yet enacted comprehensive legislation to protect individuals' personal data, with the exception of Argentina, Mexico, Chile and Uruguay. Others (including Brazil, Bolivia, Colombia, Costa Rica, Guatemala and Peru) are currently considering enacting a comprehensive data protection law, or are updating their weak legal safeguards, as in the case of Chile. Governments' demands for the collection and storage of more information, including biometric data in national identification cards or passports, jeopardises individuals' privacy and security, creating a database that has the potential to locate and track people with a high degree of accuracy. Plans for these sorts of databases are currently underway in several countries. A serious discussion is needed about the policy implications of covert surveillance programmes in Latin America and their impact on citizens' privacy and freedom of expression rights. ❐

40(2): 116/123
DOI: 10.1177/0306422011411270
www.indexoncensorship.org

Katitza Rodríguez is the international rights director at the Electronic Frontier Foundation

STRICTLY PERSONAL

What does a corporation have in common with a person? **Marc Rotenberg** examines a test case for transparency in the US

It is a busy time for open government law in the United States. As the US Congress considers new legislation to strengthen and update the federal Freedom of Information Act (FOIA), the US Supreme Court has recently issued two opinions that point toward greater transparency in the federal government. Meanwhile, academics in Wisconsin are fretting over the strategic use of the state freedom of information legislation (FOI) by the Republican Party to uncover private emails of university professors critical of the state's governor. And questions remain about the 'political processing' of FOIA requests.

The Supreme Court's support for open government is of particular interest to litigators and journalists and appears to defy the common view that the US high court is deferential to secrecy and corporate power. In one of the most remarkable opinions of the last few years, the court was asked to consider whether corporations have a 'personal privacy' right that would block the disclosure of government information that might otherwise be available to the public.

The case arose following an investigation by the US Federal Communications Commission of AT&T's billing practices. In the course of the investigation, the federal agency obtained detailed information from AT&T that was subject to disclosure under the FOIA. But whether particular documents would be released, or released in part, would depend upon the various open government exemptions that the agency might assert.

The case got into the courts when one of AT&T's competitors asked the commission to disclose the records of the investigation pursuant to the open government law. As required by the federal law, the agency processed the request, identified the relevant documents, and applied various exemptions. Some materials were withheld because they contained trade secrets or other proprietary business information, a recognised exemption in the US FOI law. Other records were withheld because they concerned personal information about employees of the company, another recognised exemption.

But then AT&T presented a novel argument in support of further withholding. The company said that it too was entitled to the 'personal privacy' exemption because a corporation is a 'legal person' and 'personal' is merely the adjectival form of the noun. AT&T's argument became more interesting still when the company reminded all that it was not just individuals who were entitled to make requests under the US open government law, but all 'persons', which AT&T helpfully pointed out included 'an individual, partnership, corporation, association, or public or private organisation other than an agency'. According to the company, AT&T was not just a person in the general legal sense, it was also one in the specific language of the FOIA.

A federal appeals court agreed with AT&T's logic, and held in its favour. The case was appealed, the Supreme Court agreed to hear the case, and suddenly open government advocates were reading dictionaries and calling up their old teachers to ask if AT&T could really be correct. In addition to the linguistic quandary presented in *FCC v AT&T*, the case was interesting also as the Supreme Court had ruled just a year earlier in *Citizens United* that corporations had broad free speech rights under the First Amendment. That decision scuttled large sections of the campaign finances law enacted by Congress. To some, an outcome in favour of AT&T seemed pre-ordained.

But courts often surprise people and the Supreme Court surprised at least a few people when it thoroughly rejected AT&T's argument and held that the 'personal privacy' exemption in the US federal open government law was for persons who actually put on clothes and sit down for dinner.

Chief Justice Roberts, who wrote for a unanimous court, noted at the outset that 'adjectives typically reflect the meaning of corresponding nouns, but not always'. Quoting Webster's dictionary, the chief justice observed that 'corny can mean using familiar and stereotyped formulas believed to appeal

Credit: Kjell Nilsson-Makl/Cartoon Stock

to the unsophisticated, which has little to do with corn, the seeds of any of the cereal grasses used for food'; and while 'crank is a part of an axis bent at right angles, cranky can mean given to fretful fussiness'.

The court looked at the uses of the phrase in other settings as well as the legislative history of the provision. There was just not much support that favoured AT&T's position. The Supreme Court noted that it had previously described that same provision as involving an 'individual's right of privacy'. And the court observed that for the law enforcement exemption that also includes the phrase 'personal privacy', an important government memorandum explained that the provision 'pertains to the privacy interests of individuals'.

The justices ended the opinion with a smile: 'The protection in FOIA against disclosure of law enforcement information on the ground that it would constitute an unwarranted invasion of personal privacy does not extend to corporations', wrote the chief justice. 'We trust that AT&T will not take it personally.'

My organisation EPIC, which supports both personal privacy and government transparency, had filed a friend of the court brief on behalf of legal scholars and technical experts in which we discussed the meaning of 'personal privacy', as well as the use of the phrase in an extensive survey of US privacy laws we put together. We warned the Supreme Court that if it upheld the lower court's view of 'personal privacy', the decision would 'stand as an outlier, untethered to common understanding, legal scholarship, technical methods, or privacy law'. EPIC also said that 'the decision below is contrary to widespread understanding, and almost nonsensical'. The Supreme Court seemed to agree.

The solicitor general, representing the administration of President Obama, also filed a brief in support of the petitioner, the Federal Communications Commission. The Department of Justice would have represented the federal agency before the court under any scenario. But the additional participation by the solicitor general gave the case a further nudge in the direction of greater openness, though there was an awkward moment when the government's advocate before the court argued that in this case the justices should favour transparency, while in another FOIA before the court, greater secrecy should be favoured. Several open government advocates winced.

Of course, it is possible to read both too much and too little into this opinion on privacy and government transparency. The decision did not unsettle the earlier *Citizens United* opinion, as that case turned on the court's view of the First Amendment and the *FCC v AT&T* case is about the language in a particular federal statute. The decision also did not mark a new direction from the court's mostly conservative views on corporate liability and labour rights.

Still, it remains noteworthy and may carry some insight into the purpose of FOIA laws, as well as the relationship between privacy and open government, that would be helpful for journalists and advocates around the world.

First, the text of an open government statute matters, but more important still is the purpose of the law. AT&T presented a clever, hyper-technical argument. But it was ultimately unsuccessful because a coherent understanding of the US open government law, which already provided an exemption for business secrets, could not reasonably also include an exemption for a 'personal privacy' right of corporations. No dictionaries need be revised as a result of this decision.

Second, even though many entities may properly seek records under an open records law, how the exemptions in the law are to be applied is an entirely separate question. Government may choose to give organisations and corporations the same right to access records as it does to individuals. But when it comes to determining whether information should be withheld, it is fully appropriate to distinguish these entities.

Third, the court's opinion in *AT&T v FCC* reminds us also that there is a critical distinction between personal privacy and corporate secrecy. Individuals have privacy rights that are fundamental rights and derived from the same international human rights documents that also safeguard freedom of expression. There is simply no comparable claim for corporations. Government may choose in some limited circumstances to establish such exemptions, recognising, for example, that an FOI law might be abused by a company seeking to uncover the trade secrets of a competitor. But such exemptions have a narrow purpose that should not be confused with the interest in safeguarding the rights of individuals.

Beyond the court's opinion in *FCC v AT&T*, there is also the court's decision in *Milner v Navy* that limits the scope of one of the exemptions – 'high' (b)(2) – and should make government information more widely available. The court sided with a FOIA requester who charged that the Department of the Navy had improperly withheld government maps describing the location of explosive material, an environmental concern, as human resources materials. Two points for government transparency.

There are also efforts under way in Congress to improve the processing of FOIA requests. But there are new concerns too. Federal agencies, notably the Department of Homeland Security, are notifying the White House of FOIA requests that might have political ramifications. These agencies provide information to the political appointees about the identities and interests of FOIA requesters. The practical consequence is to delay the processing of requests and to subject the requests to greater scrutiny. This is completely outside the federal law and contrary to a central tenet of the US FOI, repeatedly emphasised by the Supreme Court, that neither the identity of the requester nor the purpose of the request should be considered in the processing of FOIA requests. The House Oversight Committee recently held hearings to look into this issue in more detail.

In another development, employees of public universities in the state of Wisconsin learned that their emails could be subject to disclosure under the state open government law. This followed a political battle with the new governor and efforts by the governor's party to uncover the communications of university professors critical of the new programmes. As with the controversy over the political processing of FOIA requests, the bedrock presumption that neither the identity of the requester nor the purpose of the requester should be taken into account when assessing the validity of an open government request is the starting point for the legal analysis. But the Wisconsin case does raise an interesting question – should an FOI exemption that might protect personal communications as part of a privacy interest be strengthened further to safeguard intellectual freedom? Should courts or lawmakers specifically recognise the value of academic freedom in the FOI world? It might seem odd to grant academics, often users of the FOI to uncover materials for books and scholarly articles, an exemption for their own deliberations.

Still, it is hardly inconsistent for freedom of information laws, intended to promote government transparency while safeguarding personal privacy, to recognise the special place of academic freedom. And the purposeful intrusion, by means of the FOIA, into the private thoughts of those seeking to organise against the party in power should set off alarms.

Perhaps some things should be taken personally. ❐

40(2): 125/130
DOI: 10.1177/0306422011410652
www.indexoncensorship.org

Marc Rotenberg is president of the Electronic Privacy Information Center (EPIC) in Washington, DC and co-editor of *Litigation under the Federal Open Government Laws*. He teaches Information Privacy Law at Georgetown University Law Center

STRANGE FRUIT

The Indian government's pursuit of BlackBerry reveals inconsistencies in its policy on privacy and security. **Prashant Iyengar** reports

Over the past few years, the stand-off between Research in Motion (RIM), the owners of BlackBerry, and the Indian government has been keeping telecom policy-watchers entertained. Email, web traffic and PIN messages are encrypted on BlackBerry devices and cannot be intercepted by security agencies. The government has been insistent in its demands that RIM make facilities available to enable interception in real time. Failure to do so would, it alleges, threaten India's national security. Furthermore, politicians point out, all other telecom operators in India have complied with this demand. The clinching argument, so far as the government is concerned, is that China, Saudi Arabia and the UAE have been reported to have access, and India does not want to be excluded. RIM responded to these demands first by denying that it was technologically possible, and then by offering half-measures which have not impressed the government.

Like the fruit which only grows in cold climates, BlackBerry mobile phones are rare in India. More than 800m Indians use mobile phones, while there are only a million BlackBerry users. So why is this controversy important in India?

There are a million BlackBerry users in India – and more than 800m mobile phones
Ahmadabad, India, 27 August 2010
Credit: Ajit Solanki/AP

BlackBerry services were launched by several telecom networks in India in 2004. No concerns were raised by the government about intercepting data until 2008. In March that year, Tata Teleservices (TTSL), a new telecom service provider, sought permission from the Department of Telecommunications (DoT) to offer BlackBerry services on its network. The Unified Access Services licence (UASL), mandatory for all telecom providers since 2004, contains a clause forbidding them from employing bulk encryption equipment in their network unless prior approval is obtained from the DoT.

Curiously, none of the major service providers – including the state-run BSNL which had been offering BlackBerry services since 2004 – had considered it necessary to obtain permission under this clause. A further clause requires licensees to 'provide the necessary facilities for continuous monitoring of the system'. However, inspection would 'ordinarily be carried out after reasonable notice except in circumstances where giving such a notice will defeat the very purpose of the inspection'.

The DoT not only declined TTSL permission to offer BlackBerry on the grounds that 'BlackBerry services do not have scope for lawful interception', but then issued instructions to all mobile service providers asking them 'not to connect or provide/run certain BlackBerry services unless the required monitoring systems are in place'. This set in motion a three-year period of hectic dialogue, first between the telecom operators and the government, and then directly between Research in Motion and the government.

In January, RIM bowed to pressure and offered the government access to consumer services, including its messenger services. However, the company still insisted that it was technologically impossible to offer interception of encrypted communications that travelled over their corporate enterprise servers, since these were controlled entirely by their clients. The government has termed this solution unsatisfactory and insisted that RIM turn over the keys to corporate email services. RIM has sought a period of two years to develop a solution that would enable interception of their enterprise email. The government has neither rejected nor acquiesced to this demand.

In March, an article appeared in TechDirt suggesting that the government was ready to soften its stance and assume responsibility for building technologies for intelligence agencies for monitoring and interception purposes. At the same time, the media reported that RIM had been given till the end of the month to fully comply with the government's requirements or face a ban. That date has passed without any further action.

Anyone familiar with the Indian state will know that it has an indifferent record of enforcing strict compliance within the letter of the law. Our courts do not, for instance, insist that evidence be obtained lawfully by police officers, by strictly following procedures laid down in the Criminal Procedure Code. Instead, illegal searches and wiretapping have been held to be mere irregularities, and evidence obtained may still be admissible.

Another regrettable feature of the Indian criminal justice apparatus is the failure of the intelligence machinery at all levels. Despite the heavy investment and rhetoric about the deployment of advanced surveillance technologies, rarely have these been useful in preventing crimes. The Mumbai attack in 2008, when Pakistani militants took guests hostage in the Taj Hotel, itself presents a sorry case study in how the government and security agencies sat on credible intelligence reports about imminent terrorist attacks. It is not the inadequacy of intelligence mechanisms in India, but the unwillingness of security agencies to act upon such information that has led to the persistence of crime.

The government's stern insistence on compliance in the case of BlackBerry therefore seems somewhat incongruous with both how the state normally operates and its demonstrated incapacity to deploy technology effectively for purposes of national security. The DoT's disproportionate position in its dealings with RIM may partly also be the fallout of the Mumbai attack (some of the militants were BlackBerry users). Envy might be a motive too: other countries have been more successful at arm-twisting RIM into compliance. Last August, BlackBerry agreed to the monitoring of email and instant messaging data services in Saudi Arabia. UAE has now banned individuals and small businesses from using the most secure BlackBerry settings, a retreat from its previous threat of a total ban. The restrictions will also apply to all phone companies in the country. In India, RIM now appears to be paying the price for its initial obdurate stance, whereas most other telecom service providers have facilitated government monitoring. Nokia, for example, set up an enterprise server in India last year to enable government monitoring.

In terms of consumer privacy, the BlackBerry controversy does not significantly worsen the average citizen's existent right to privacy. Theoretically, all mobile users are already susceptible to interception by the DoT. The opening up of BlackBerry users to government surveillance merely countervails the relatively enhanced privacy of a small group. Telecom service provider Reliance Communications told the supreme court earlier this year that 30,000 interceptions took place yearly between 2006 and 2010. It may be ultimately futile to rely on a technological solution to fix what is clearly a systemic problem.

It will be interesting to see how the government now deals with online services such as Gmail and Skype which employ higher encryption standards than permissible under law. A number of factors may shield them from government action: first, the fact that other branches of the government – such as the Reserve Bank of India, which regulates the banking industry, and SEBI, which regulates stock trading – prescribe and require high browser encryption in excess of the 40bit encryption permitted by the DoT, for operations that fall within their purview. Attempting to enforce strict adherence to their encryption norms might draw the DoT into an inter-departmental fight, in which it would be sparring far above its weight.

Second, regardless of what the policy requires them to do, Google has, of its own volition, proven to be compliant with official requests for taking down material and assisting in criminal investigations. This may prove to be an additional factor in their favour. Finally, the ubiquity of Gmail and Skype (in contrast to BlackBerry's marginality) may shield them against any stiff measures, as the government has on occasion altered its policy in the face of its inability to regulate popular technologies. This happened in the early part of the last decade when the DoT was forced to permit Voice over Internet Protocol (VOIP) calls between PCs in the face of the growing popularity of such software. So there is some hope yet that the government may revise its prescriptions on encryption technology, which would protect Gmail and Skype. ❐

40(2): 132/136
DOI: 10.1177/0306422011411631
www.indexoncensorship.org

Prashant Iyengar is a practising lawyer based in Bangalore. He is a consultant at the Center for Internet and Society and lead researcher for Privacy India, an affiliate of Privacy International

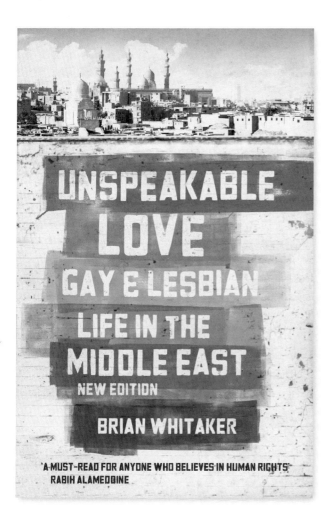

IND

IND

EX

EX

A censorship chronicle incorporating privacy stories from Agence France Presse (AFP), Arab News, BBC, Brothersoft, Business Review Europe, *Der Spiegel*, *Economist*, Electronic Frontier Foundation (EFF), Electronic Privacy Information Center, European Digital Rights, *Financial Times*, *Guardian*, *Latin American Herald Tribune*, MSNBC, *New Statesman*, *New York Times*, Open Net Initiative, *Pakistan Tribune*, Radio Free Asia, Radio Free Europe/Radio Liberty (RFE/RL), Reporters sans frontières (RSF), Softpedia, *Taipei Times*, Techradar.com, Télam, *Telegraph*, *Time*, *USA Today*, *Wall Street Journal*, ZDNet, Zee News and other organisations affiliated with the International Freedom of Expression Exchange (IFEX)

Argentina

In February 2011, **Felipe and Marcela Noble Herrera**, adopted children of one of the richest women in the country, lost their legal challenge to the country's DNA laws, which forced them to give DNA samples in an attempt to establish their true parentage. In May 2010, following the pair's refusal to provide samples, their house was raided, they were strip-searched and samples from clothing and toothbrushes were taken. A 2009 law gave the courts power to forcibly obtain DNA if someone refuses to submit to a blood test. The law's origin dates back to the 1970s and 1980s when left-wing activists were kidnapped, tortured and imprisoned by the military dictatorship. Many of those detained were young couples with either newborns or mothers expecting a child; babies were taken away and given to military or police officials to bring up as their own. The government that followed the military dictatorship set up a National Bank of Genetic Data, where grandparents and relatives of the missing children contribute samples of their DNA for identification purposes. Although campaigners have been working to identify the children of the disappeared, not all of them want to know about their biological parents. (BBC, Télam, *Time*)

Armenia

On 23 November 2010, the constitutional court ruled that wiretapping by police was unlawful. A 2005 amendment to the country's criminal code allowed the **monitoring of private communications** without a court order if one of the parties involved was a member of a law enforcement agency. It is thought that the National Security Service had intercepted telephone calls of at least one opposition politician, and there has been widespread criticism of the legislation on behalf of journalists and activists. (RFE/RL)

Australia

Northern Territory News journalist **Justin O'Brien** complained to the Northern Territory ombudsman on 11 November 2010 that police had illegally accessed his phone records in an attempt to discover the identity of a police officer who had leaked information to him. Police Commissioner John McRoberts insists that his force acted within the law. (ABC)

On 3 December 2010, the Australian Federal Police (AFP) ceased its investigation into Google's collection of private **wi-fi data** through its Street View cars. The police stated that because the potential breach of privacy laws by Google was inadvertent, it would not be an efficient use of resources to pursue the matter further. Under Australian law, privacy breaches must be done with intent to be prosecutable. The federal government initially referred the case to the AFP on 3 June 2010. (Softpedia, ZDNet)

Bangladesh

On 20 February 2011, the Supreme Court sacked a judge after finding him guilty of installing a hidden camera inside his **colleague's bedroom**. Iliyas Rahman, a lower court judge, admitted committing the act after being 'influenced by adventure movies'. (Zee News)

Brazil

Cables originating from the US embassy in Brasilia and released by WikiLeaks in December 2010 led privacy advocates to raise concerns that the **Olympic Games in Brazil** in 2016 will be used as an opportunity to increase public surveillance. Citing examples from Athens and Beijing, advocates argue that temporary surveillance measures are often made permanent after the Games end. The WikiLeaks cables also highlight how the US influenced security and information-sharing strategies. (EFF)

Canada

A court ruled on 19 October 2010 that Google violated the **privacy rights of citizens** when it introduced Street View. The privacy commissioner stated that collection of data in the run up to the launch of the service had been done without consent and ordered Google to delete all confidential data by 1 February 2011. (*Guardian*)

China

Google accused the Chinese government of hacking into **Gmail users' accounts** on 21 March 2011. The claim followed complaints from Gmail users over a number of weeks, when disruption to email services coincided with parliamentary sessions in Beijing. There was speculation that it was at least in part connected to uprisings in the Middle East and that political activists were being targeted. **Microblogging sites** reported similar disruptions. Also blocked in the country was an application Google set up to help those affected by the tsunami and earthquake in Japan. In September 2010, Google warned its email users that it suspected there had been widespread attempts to access personal mail accounts from internet addresses within the country. (Radio Free Asia)

Throughout August 2010, engineers installed Skynet electronic surveillance equipment in **internet cafes** in Tibet. Engineers attended individual sites to meet a 31 August 2010 deadline set by the government. Similar systems were installed in Ganzi in Sichuan Province and plans were underway to cover the Batang region. Officials stated that the monitoring devices increased public safety and supported economic and social initiatives. (Radio Free Asia)

Colombia

The hearing of former President Álvaro Uribe came before Congress's investigative committee on 3 November 2010. The previous year, the president was accused of using DAS, the country's domestic intelligence agency, to **illegally wiretap opposition judges, politicians and journalists**. Uribe denied any knowledge of the situation, but former intelligence officials directly implicated him in the conspiracy. An investigation by the Inter-American Commission on Human Rights began in March 2011. At the same time, in November 2010, Belgium began its own investigation into claims that DAS illegally intercepted phone calls in Belgium. According to reports, the agency also monitored European NGOs and the European Parliament. (*Economist*, *Latin American Herald Tribune*)

France

On 17 March 2011, the French data protection agency CNIL fined Google €100,000 (US$143,200) over its **data collecting** practices for its Google Maps, Street View and Latitude services. The company collected wi-fi data, including emails, without the permission of users. According to CNIL, although Google made a commitment to stop collecting wi-fi data with its Google cars and to erase the content it had collected in error, the company had not stopped using data identifying private individuals' wi-fi access points. (Associated Press, BBC, Brothersoft)

The French Association of Internet Community Services lodged a complaint against the government over a new regulation pertaining to **data retention** in April 2011. The law requires companies to store extensive data on service users, including names, passwords and telephone numbers; companies are also obliged to share this information with authorities when required. The association, a group of more than 20 internet businesses including Facebook and eBay, argued that the government failed to consult with the European Commission prior to passing the law. The decree, which came into effect on 1 March, also requires internet service providers to store personal data for one year. Since any change to the data automatically restarts the year-long period, a routine action such as changing a password means that ISPs are forced to store a large amount of data in an unencrypted form for an indefinite period of time. (RSF, *Telegraph*)

Germany

Legislation passed in August 2010 made it illegal for companies to collect **information about potential employees** using social networking websites. The bill also made it illegal for companies to use **video surveillance** in some areas of offices, including toilets, changing rooms and break rooms. Under the legislation, companies are required to inform employees if their telephones and emails are being monitored for any reason. (*Der Spiegel*)

Prosecutors charged a man with spying on ethnic **Uighur exiles** on behalf of China's intelligence services in April 2011. The charges relate to information that the defendant allegedly passed to Chinese authorities between April 2008 and October 2009. Germany is home to a significant number of Uighurs who have repeatedly called for greater freedom and tolerance in China. (MSNBC)

Indonesia

Research In Motion (RIM), the company that produces the BlackBerry smart phone, announced on 11 January 2011 that it is to filter pornographic content on its phones in Indonesia 'as soon as possible'. It will be the first time the company has applied **internet filtering** in any country. RIM met with government officials on 17 January to discuss the issue. The move comes after the government ordered ISPs to block customers from visiting websites containing pornographic content. The ban presents technical problems as corporate BlackBerry data traffic is heavily encrypted and routed through a gateway that telecommunications providers cannot access. (*Wall Street Journal*)

International

It was revealed on 20 April 2011 that the Apple iPhone records **phone users'** movements and locations, uploading the information to the owner's personal computer when the two devices are synchronised. Privacy advocates raised concerns because, although police can obtain information about an individual's whereabouts and recent locations in many countries, they must do this via a court order; the Apple products retain this information routinely and it can be obtained by any one with access to the mobile user's phone or computer. Apple's iPad tracks and records locations in a similar way. (*Guardian*)

Israel

The army revealed in November 2010 that authorities used Facebook accounts to obtain **information about young women** who have tried to avoid military service by pretending to be religious. Around 1000 women were identified through photos that showed them eating in non-kosher restaurants, accepting invitations to parties on a Friday night, or wearing revealing clothing. Israeli law allows women who sign a declaration saying they eat only kosher food and do not work on the Sabbath to be exempt from military service. (AFP)

Italy

Three Google executives were given suspended six-month jail sentences on 24 February 2010. Chief legal officer **David Drummond**, chief privacy counsel **Peter Fleischer** and former chief financial officer **George Reyes** were charged with violating privacy after a video clip showing schoolboys bullying an autistic boy was posted on a Google forum in 2006. The ruling led to a debate about whether online companies should be legally responsible for content and what their role as monitors of this content should be. The video was removed in 2006, two months after its original posting. Google is appealing. (*Telegraph*, *Time*)

Kyrgyzstan

On 23 May 2010, an investigation began into allegations that foreign governments had **wiretapped conversations** between members of the country's interim government. According to a high-ranking official, secret services in Kazakhstan, Uzbekistan, Russia, and the United States were guilty of recording online conversations concerning corruption. (RFE/RL)

Malaysia

A female patient won a court case against doctors who photographed intimate parts of her body prior to her medical operation. In September 2010, a judge ruled that doctors must obtain consent before taking **photographs.** (*Indian*)

Pakistan

Because the country's law books do not include specific legislation concerning privacy, news organisations were free to include **private details about a rape case** in December 2010 reports. Media organisations reported on comments made by police officers, personal details about the victim and interviews that discussed her 'character'. (*Pakistan Tribune*)

Russia

The FSB, Russia's domestic spy agency, called for the closure of several popular internet services on 8 April 2011. Although the Kremlin distanced itself from the comments, there were mounting fears that the state could impose some form of restriction on the use of **encrypted technology** such as Skype, Gmail and Hotmail. According to analysts, the FSB has raised fears that foreign encryption prevents them from accessing information that may be crucial to national security. (*Telegraph*)

South Korea

South Korea's police authority claimed on 6 January 2011 that Google violated the country's privacy laws when its Street View cars mistakenly collected **personal information** such as emails and passwords. Google apologised for the incident and insisted that it had cooperated fully with authorities. It is not yet clear whether the government will prosecute the internet company. (*Guardian*)

Spain

On 17 January 2010, the Spanish Data Protection Authority (AEPD) accused Google of invading **customers' privacy**. Arguing that the company was in breach of the 'right to be forgotten', the AEPD ordered the search engine to remove more than 100 links to Spanish articles that contained information on specific individuals. Google maintained that the ruling infringed on freedom of expression rights and will fight the case in court. It also argued that since it was not the publisher of the articles and only acted as an intermediary via its search engine, it should not be obliged to remove the links. It is thought that the case will be referred to the European Court of Justice in Luxembourg. (European Digital Rights, OpenNet Initiative)

Switzerland

On 4 April 2011, the Federal Court in Berne ordered Google to ensure that every face and licence plate be blurred before being uploaded to the Swiss version of Google Street View. The automated blurring process successfully blurs 99% of the relevant content but the court ruled that the process should be a manual one in order to avoid error and protect the **privacy of citizens.** The ruling stems from a lawsuit brought by a Swiss privacy watchdog in 2009. In its judgment, the court stated that privacy concerns should not be compromised in the interests of saving money. (*Business Review Europe*)

Trinidad and Tobago

On 12 November 2011, Prime Minister Kamla Persad-Bissessar revealed to parliament that the Security Intelligence Agency (SIA) had been illegally tapping telephones and intercepting emails for 15 years. Targets have included **politicians, judges, trade unionists, entertainment personalities and journalists**. The operation was initiated by a previous government and the prime minister was quoted as saying she had not been aware of the violations. In December 2010, the government passed the Interception of Communications Act, which makes it legal to wiretap on security grounds. (RSF)

United Kingdom

On 10 May 2011, the European Court of Human Rights rejected former head of Formula One World Championship **Max Mosley**'s attempts to tighten privacy laws. The court ruled that newspapers are not required to notify individuals before aspects of their private lives are revealed in the media. The Strasbourg court ruled that there had not been a breach of Article 8 of the European Convention on Human Rights, which guarantees the right to privacy, and that pre-notification would have a negative impact on journalism. Revelations of Mosley's sex life were revealed in the *News of the World* in 2008. The High Court in England awarded Mosley damages that year. (*Guardian, Telegraph*)

The High Court lifted an anonymity order relating to a prominent businessman on 19 May 2011 after a politician named him, citing parliamentary privilege. A legal team working for ex-Royal Bank of Scotland director **Sir Fred Goodwin** had secured an injunction so that newspapers were unable to publish details about his private life. (BBC)

After Twitter and other social network websites named individuals who had issued gagging orders in April 2011, a **footballer** involved in one such injunction was named in Parliament on 23 May, leading to the publication of his name in the mainstream media. In April 2010, a committee including judges, legal experts and media representatives began a review of the use of injunctions and super-injunctions to restrict reporting on prominent figures. (*Metro, Telegraph*)

The Crown Prosecution Service (CPS) ruled on 8 April 2011 that British Telecom and Phorm would not face prosecution over their **interception of internet traffic**. In 2006, it emerged that the browsing patterns of 18,000 BT customers had been monitored without their knowledge in an effort to help software company Phorm design a more targeted online advertising mechanism. The CPS stated that as there was insufficient evidence to bring prosecution under the Regulation of Investigatory Powers Act, any action would be against the public interest. The case exposed various loopholes in UK privacy laws, which the European Commission then asked the Home Office to address. (*Telegraph*)

The Home Office agreed in November 2010 to meet civil liberties groups as part of a consultation into UK **interception laws**. The European Commission ordered a review of data laws after it was revealed that the UK had no legal redress for citizens who suspect that their web browsing or email has been monitored without permission. (BBC)

Plans to fine a county council that faxed details of a child sex abuse case to a member of the public were announced on 24 November 2010. Hertfordshire County Council was handed down a fine after it was found to be in breach of the Data Protection Act. A Sheffield-based company was also fined for losing an unencrypted laptop containing the details of thousands of people. The fines were the first brought by the country's Information Commissioner in connection with **data protection violations**. (BBC)

Spanish legal authorities took steps to prosecute the *Daily Mail* in early November 2010 after the paper was accused of invading the privacy of a **minor**. Following a Seville prosecutor's request for media outlets to stop publishing photographs of the family home of a 10-year-old girl who had given birth to a baby fathered by her 13-year-old cousin, the newspaper published a photograph of the couple on 2 November. Prosecutors also stated their intentions to take legal action against a Cadiz newspaper that printed photographs of the baby. (*Guardian*)

A school in Staffordshire was criticised for its use of closed circuit television (CCTV) in January 2011. Tamworth school allegedly used CCTV footage to fine **pupils** caught smoking on school premises, but privacy campaigners argued that the data protection code of practice clearly states that the public must be warned if security cameras are to be used for non-security purposes. (BBC)

England footballer **Peter Crouch** accused the *Sun* of invading his privacy on 17 April 2011 after it was revealed that his girlfriend Abbey Clancy was pregnant before members of their family were informed. Clancy accused reporters of following her to the clinic and subsequently eavesdropping on a private conversation in a restaurant. (*New Statesman*)

On 16 December 2010, actor **Matt Lucas** won substantial undisclosed damages from the *Daily Mail* after the paper published a story following his ex-partner's death. According to Lucas's law firm, Schillings, the article was an intrusion into his suffering and an invasion of his privacy. (*Guardian*)

On 8 April 2011, Rupert Murdoch's News International admitted liability in the country's **celebrity phone hacking** scandal. It offered to pay compensation to eight public figures whose voicemails and private messages were intercepted on behalf of *News of the World*. News International had previously denied all involvement in the scandal and had maintained that the private detective at the heart of the scandal, Glenn Mulcaire, was not its agent when he committed the hackings. (*Financial Times*)

Senior *News of the World* journalist James Weatherup was arrested on 14 April 2011 by police investigating claims that the newspaper had hacked into **celebrities' phone records.** He was the third current *News of the World* reporter to be arrested in connection with the investigation. Ian Edmondson was suspended on 5 January 2011 and arrested on 5 April 2011. Neville Thurlbeck was also arrested on 5 April 2011. Both men were released on police bail and will appear in court in September. The police re-opened its investigation after receiving new information on the case. (BBC)

United States of America

On 31 March 2010, a San Francisco district court found that the US government had illegally wiretapped a US-based **Islamic charity's** telephone calls in 2004, breaching the Foreign Intelligence Surveillance Act (FISA). FISA requires the government to obtain a warrant before any surveillance operation. It was the first case in which the National Security Agency's 'warrantless wiretapping' was found to be illegal. (Arabnews, EFF)

It was announced on 30 March 2011 that Google must undergo independent privacy audits for a period of 20 years on the grounds that it wrongfully used information from **Gmail** to create its social network Buzz. The US Federal Trade Commission (FTC) accused Google of violating 'its own privacy promises'. Particularly controversial was a feature that publicly listed Gmail users' regular contacts. Buzz used the option as a default setting for profiles, though individual users could change the settings. (BBC, Brothersoft)

On 22 March 2011, a federal district judge ruled that Google had made adequate provisions for readers' privacy in its plans for an online library, which will be launched in 2015. A number of writers and privacy advocates argued that the settlement between Google and the Authors Guild of America, the Association of American Publishers and big publishing firms did not adequately protect the privacy of **Google Books users** and that they were entitled to further protection from government collection of personal data. Campaigners had advocated for better copyright law to accommodate for the mass digitisation of books. (BBC, EFF)

Privacy advocates appealed to the House Oversight Subcommittee on National Security to suspend the Transportation Security Administration's (TSA) body scanner programme at US airports on 16 March 2011. Witnesses giving evidence at the hearing claimed the process was only minimally effective and was in violation of **privacy law.** The technology allows for detailed, three-dimensional images of individuals, data that is then retained by the TSA. (Electronic Privacy Information Center, MSNBC)

Federal government plans to build back doors into **all communications systems,** including encryption software, social networking sites and email services, were revealed on 27 September 2010. Under the bill, peer-to-peer software developers will be ordered to alter their services to allow for interception and unscrambling of encrypted messages. The Obama administration stated that the new law was required because of criminals and terrorists' widespread use of the internet. Communication service providers that have business relations in the country but are based outside the US will be required to comply with the proposed legislation. Privacy advocates warned of the dangers of introducing such legislation, pointing out that unlawful spying on behalf of criminals and governments has been made possible through exploiting the 'lawful intercept' systems built into already-existing laws. (EFF, *New York Times*)

Following the closure of a magazine in February 2010, the Federal Trade Commission announced that the sale of **personal data** associated with the publication could be in violation of federal law. When *XY* magazine filed for bankruptcy, creditors requestered a list of registered users from the publication. (BBC)

US Congress voted on 14 February 2011 to extend the provisions of the Patriot Act until 8 December 2011, extending some of the Federal Bureau of Investigation's powers. Provisions allow for the seizure of 'tangible' assets relevant to security investigations, **wiretapping of suspects** who are not US citizens and who are not affiliated with any foreign power, as well as 'roving wiretaps' in situations where suspects change service providers. (*New York Times, USA Today*)

Vietnam

In March 2011, Google claimed that malicious software was being used to target **anti-government blogs and websites.** Google alleged that the malware installed itself when users downloaded software that enabled Vietnamese characters. The software also raised concerns as privacy analysts pointed out that it could be used to acquire private information on users. (BBC, *Taipei Times*)

Edited by Natasha Schmidt
Compiled by Laura MacPhee, Saad Mustafa and Mohammad Zaman
DOI: 10.1177/0306422011410164

FACES OF POWER

Anthony Lester on blasphemy

Fiction from Libya

Demonstration in support of Pakistan's blasphemy laws, Karachi, 9 January 2011
Credit: Akhtar Soomro/Reuters

FIGHTING WORDS

It's time that law makers stepped in to tackle the growing conflicts worldwide between freedom of expression and freedom of religion, argues **Anthony Lester**

In an age of 24-hour global news and comment, any attacks on religious beliefs and practices are instantly magnified and transmitted around the world, sometimes with deadly consequences.

Take the case of Pastor Terry Jones, a notorious evangelical bigot who has courted publicity and preached hatred against Islam from his Dove World Outreach Center in Florida. This culminated, on 20 March, in a supervised 'trial' during which the Quran was found guilty of 'crimes against humanity', soaked in petrol, and set alight in the glare of filmed publicity. Two weeks later, mobs in Afghanistan attacked the UN Mission in Mazar-e-Sharif, killing seven of its staff, and next day in Kandahar at least ten more people were killed in a second day of protests. Jones has since threatened to put the Prophet Mohammed on 'trial' in his next 'day of judgment'.

He first threatened to burn the Quran on last year's anniversary of the 11 September 2001 attacks on the US, and was widely condemned across the Muslim world. He made plans to come to Britain to speak to the English Defence League against what he called 'the evils and destructiveness of

Islam', but the Home Secretary banned him from coming on the grounds that his presence would not be conducive to the public good.

Incidents like these create perplexing problems for those of us who are committed to freedom of speech, religious freedom and human dignity. Despite interventions by President Obama, the US Defense Secretary Robert Gates and General Petraeus, commander of Nato forces in Afghanistan, who warned that such a stunt would endanger US lives, Jones went ahead with his 'punishment' of the Quran.

But the US government did not seek a court order forbidding him to carry out these actions, no doubt because of the First Amendment's robust protection of free speech. In light of the case *United States v Eichman* (1990), in which the American Supreme Court decided that flag burning was protected under the First Amendment, it is questionable whether such an injunction would have been granted by a US court, despite the clear and present danger of extreme violence.

We live in an age in which even satire about religious matters is hazardous, whether in Danish cartoons or a novel such as *The Satanic Verses*. When I was a student at Cambridge, EM Forster gave a lecture entitled, 'Did Jesus have a sense of humour?' and explained why he thought not. Islam is rich in humour and, in the Middle Ages, taught tolerance in Spain to followers of the other Abrahamic faiths: Christianity and Judaism. But these days a public lecture entitled 'Did the Prophet Mohammed have a sense of humour?' might well be regarded by an orthodox Muslim audience as contrary to the principles of Islamic Sharia, and as violating what the Cairo Declaration on Human Rights in Islam describes as 'the sanctities and the dignity' of the prophet.

Christian fundamentalists lack a sense of humour and a sense of proportion, too. The pressure group Christian Voice led a campaign against the BBC's airing of the production of *Jerry Springer: The Opera* in 2005 and the showing of the work in regional theatres the following year. It found the opera obscene and blasphemous. Threats were made to BBC employees and security guards had to be deployed. Happily, the BBC stood firm against these religious bullies and the attempt by Christian Voice to bring a private prosecution for blasphemy was rejected by the court.

In 2004, a rioting crowd of Sikhs stormed the Birmingham Repertory Theatre, claiming that Gurpreet Kaur Bhatti's play, *Behzti,* was an insult to their religion. No minister condemned what had happened and no prosecutions were brought. This despite the fact that the play was forced to close and the author had to go into hiding. Instead of condemning the

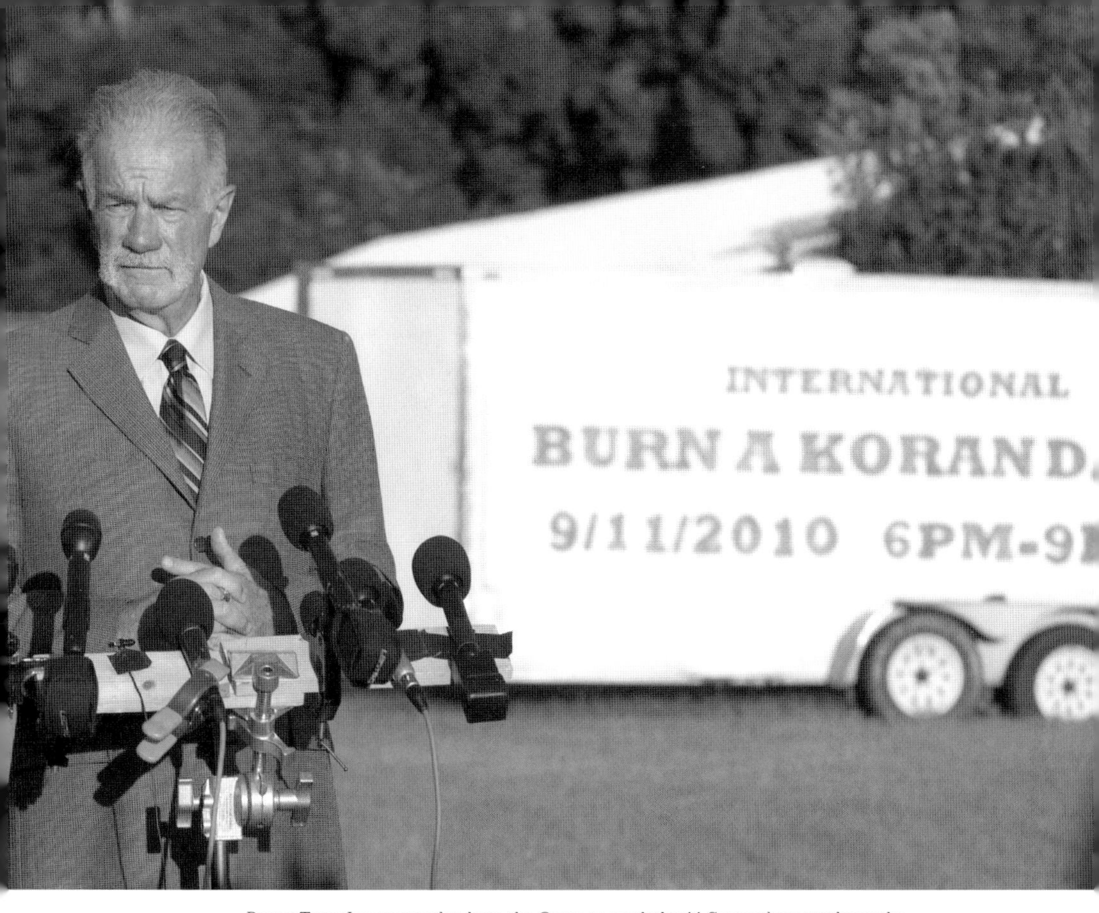

Pastor Terry Jones vowed to burn the Quran to mark the 11 September attacks on the United States, Gainesville, Florida, 8 September 2010
Credit: KeystoneUSA-ZUMA/Rex

rioters, the Home Office minister, Fiona Mactaggart, reportedly said that the free speech of the Sikh protesters was 'as important as the free speech of the artists'.

The principles of international human rights law on freedom of expression are easy to state and difficult to implement; and there are few open and plural societies where the basic principles are applied in practice. Freedom of expression is, or should be, recognised as a universal human right, and as a primary right in any democracy worthy of the name – a right without which effective rule of law is not possible. Exceptions to the right to free expression are legitimate where they aim to protect, for example, national security and public order, or the reputation and rights of others, including their human dignity. But exceptions are not justifiable merely because the expression of opinions or information shocks or offends. It is also a general principle of human rights law that any exception to the right to free expression must be narrowly interpreted in accordance with the principles of legality and proportionality.

Freedom of thought, conscience and religion are also fundamental rights, as is the equal protection of the law without discrimination, and respect for human dignity. Where these different rights and freedoms are in conflict, it is the task of the independent judiciary and the political branches of government to strike a fair balance which protects the substance of the rights at stake. No one is entitled to engage in any activity or perform any act aimed at the destruction of fundamental rights and freedoms.

Tensions about multiculturalism

Almost half a century ago, Roy Jenkins, a Home Secretary committed both to racial equality and to freedom of expression, explained what he meant by integration. 'I do not think,' he said, 'that we need in this country a "melting pot", which will turn everybody out in a common mould, as one of a series of carbon copies of someone's misplaced vision of the stereotyped Englishman.' Jenkins defined integration 'not as a flattening process of assimilation but as equality of opportunity, accompanied by cultural diversity, in an atmosphere of mutual tolerance'.

Cultural diversity is a rubbery and elusive concept and it has proved to be problematic. Like religion, culture may be a surrogate for race or ethnicity. An attack on Islam, or a Muslim, or his or her culture, may in reality be an attack on the individual's ethnic or national origin, especially since most British Muslims are of South Asian origin. When Roy Jenkins spoke in the 1960s of culture, religious identity was not in his mind, because at that stage few Commonwealth immigrants to Britain emphasised their religious identity. That is no longer the case, and the problems of multiculturalism have been compounded by the replacement of Irish terrorism by terrorist outrages committed by fanatics in the name of what they claim to be required by Islam. The problems of multiculturalism have also been exacerbated by political controversy about the nature of Britishness and British values, and the requirements of loyal British citizenship in our plural society.

This is part of the complex context in which, during the past half-century or so, British public officials and civil society have faced difficult problems about the extent of the respect to be given, in law and practice, to cultural diversity in the interests of equality, mutual tolerance, freedom of religion and freedom of speech. What was once praised as tolerant multiculturalism has come to mean excessive deference to inhuman, degrading and discriminatory practices within Britain's new ethnic and religious minorities, threatening social cohesion and equal citizenship.

When I introduced my Forced Marriage (Civil Protection) Bill, I discovered that a local education authority would not permit helpline posters to be displayed in state-funded schools for fear of offending the leaders of the local Sikh community, even though forced marriage is condemned by all religions. The problem of caste discrimination, forbidden in India but still prevalent, has been imported to Britain, and there is a power in the Equality Act 2010 to make it unlawful as part of the prohibition against ethnic discrimination. It is unclear whether the government will exercise this power in the face of opposition from the British Hindu community. A misplaced idea of multiculturalism and a desire to be popular with a particular minority should not stand in the way of forbidding caste discrimination and providing effective legal remedies for victims.

Another feature of the current situation in Britain is that many Christians believe that 'multiculturalism' amounts to a hostility to Christianity and that equality legislation is based on an extreme secularism. For example, last year, Lillian Ladele, a Christian registrar of marriages, failed to persuade the courts to exempt her from her statutory duty to register a civil partnership. On the other hand, secularists believe that the Equality Act 2010 gives too much latitude to state-funded faith schools and religious bodies and to what they see as discriminatory policies and practices based on religious doctrine and belief.

The Church of England is the established church, but Britain is a secular society. There have been recent tensions between the two, both in Parliament, during the passage of the Equality Act 2010, and in the courts. An English judge recently observed, in upholding a claim of sex discrimination by same-sex civil partners refused a double-bed hotel room, that, 'It is no longer the case that our laws must or should automatically reflect the Judaeo-Christian position' in regarding marriage as the only form of legally recognised binding relationship.

This tension was also shown in the case of Gary McFarlane, a 48-year-old Christian who was employed as a relationship counsellor. He was dismissed in March 2008 for refusing to counsel same-sex couples, and his claim to have been a victim of unlawful discrimination was rejected. On his application for permission to appeal to the Court of Appeal, he requested that his case be heard before a specially constituted court comprising the Lord Chief Justice and five Lord Justices with proven sensibility towards religious issues. A witness statement was also submitted by a former

Archbishop of Canterbury, Lord Carey, and was released to the press, accusing British courts of being anti-Christian and demanding a specialist panel of judges designated to hear cases engaging religious rights to hear the appeal and similar cases.

The Court of Appeal refused the application in April 2010, and Lord Justice Laws observed memorably that 'the conferment of any legal protection or preference upon a particular substantive moral position on the ground only that it is espoused by the adherents of a particular faith, however long its tradition, however rich its culture, is deeply unprincipled'. He continued:

> We do not live in a society where all the people share uniform religious beliefs. The precepts of any one religion – any belief system – cannot, by force of their religious origins, sound any louder in the general law than the precepts of any other. If they did, those out in the cold would be less than citizens; and our constitution would be on the way to a theocracy, which is of necessity autocratic. The law of a theocracy is dictated without option to the people, not made by their judges and governments. The individual conscience is free to accept such dictated law, but the state, if its people are to be free, has the burdensome duty of thinking for itself.

A recent judgment by the European Court of Human Rights in the Italian crucifix case (*Lautsi v Italy*, 18 March 2011) also illustrated the complex tensions between the values of religion, culture and secularism. The Grand Chamber overturned a unanimous decision by a Chamber of the Court that Italy had violated the rights of non-believing parents by requiring crucifixes to be displayed in all state-maintained school classrooms.

Soile Lautsi, a Finnish woman married to an Italian, objected that her two children had to attend a public school in northern Italy which had crucifixes in every classroom. The Chamber's decision in her favour caused outrage in the country, where the crucifix is seen as a symbol of national identity. The Chamber of the Court reasoned that: 'The Court cannot see how the display in state-school classrooms of a symbol that it is reasonable to associate with Catholicism (the majority religion in Italy) could serve the educational pluralism which is essential for the preservation of "democratic society" within the Convention meaning of that term.'

However, a majority of the Grand Chamber, while accepting that the crucifix is a religious symbol, noted the absence of evidence that the display of a religious symbol in the classroom may have an influence on pupils and added that a truly pluralist education involves exposure to a variety of different ideas including those which are different from one's own.

Flawed colonial legacy

Perplexing questions about the tension between different religions and cultures are not new. The extent to which the criminal law should accommodate different faiths, cultural values and practices was in the forefront of the minds of British imperial rulers during Queen Victoria's reign when they planned, as lawmakers for the British Raj, what became the Indian Penal Code of 1860. The men who ruled India sought to accommodate their Christian values and traditions with the traditions and values of those they ruled.

The touchstone of the Victorian codification of criminal law in British India was Jeremy Bentham's Utilitarian philosophy of reform by codification of the criminal law. Bentham was sure that universal Utilitarian principles were applicable just as much in Bengal, say, as anywhere else in the world. But he also pointed out that allowance must be made for local prejudices and customs. In Bentham's opinion, the wise legislator should be conciliatory and refrain from kindling passions that might lead to opposition to his code from the very people for whom he was legislating, while Lord Macaulay, famed architect of the draft which later resulted in the code, believed that 'government is not an institution for the propagation of religion, any more than St George's Hospital is an institution for the propagation of religion'.

The vague and sweepingly broad English common law offences of seditious, blasphemous, obscene and criminal libel fitted well within this Utilitarian philosophy of deference to multiculturalism and the preservation by the imperial rulers of public order and tranquillity. The adverse impact on the freedom of expression of the subjects of the Queen Empress was not of concern to their rulers.

The Indian Penal Code embodied these relics of English medieval ecclesiastical law and of the Court of the Star Chamber. It did so in the sweepingly broad and vague language that still characterises the criminal codes not only of India, but of Pakistan, Bangladesh, Burma, and beyond – restricting and chilling the freedom of speech and of the press. And there was no constitutional protection for free speech when the code was made.

The speech crimes in Chapter XV of the Indian Penal Code dealing with offences relating to religion include promoting or attempting to promote 'disharmony or feelings of enmity, hatred or ill-will between different

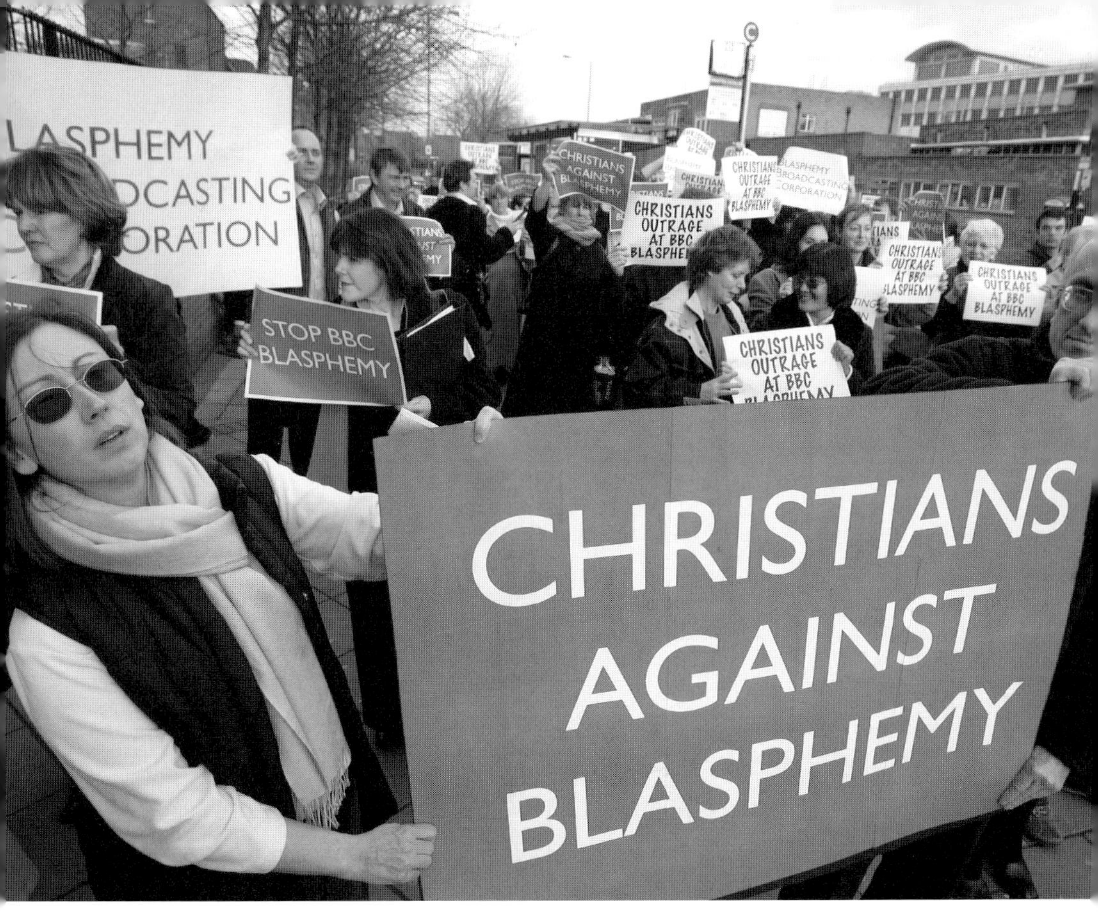

Christian organisations demonstrate against the BBC's decision to broadcast Jerry Springer – The Opera, *7 January 2005*
Credit: Stephen Hird/Reuters

religious, racial or regional groups or castes or communities' by insulting or attempting to insult the religion or the religious beliefs of that class [Section 153 (A) (1)], or deliberately and maliciously outraging the religious feelings of any class of citizens of India [Section 295A], or uttering words, etc., with deliberate intent to wound religious feelings [Section 298].

A senior advocate in India, Fali Nariman, observed that these provisions 'virtually extended by legislation the English common law of blasphemy to all religions practised in India'. And they suffer from the same vagueness and subjectivity as those archaic English offences – citing words like 'insult', 'outrage', 'wounding', 'feelings' and 'ill will', as well as the reference to the 'religious beliefs' of different 'classes'.

A leading Pakistani human rights advocate, Asma Jahangir, in her book on blasphemy in Pakistan, highlights a 1927 case involving a Hindu publisher, Raj Patel, who published a pamphlet offending the Muslim community. There was outrage among the masses and he was convicted under Section 153-A of the Indian Penal Code. The High Court quashed his conviction and ruled that Section 153-A applied to disturbing communal harmony by committing libel against a living person. Since the offensive remarks were against the Holy Prophet of Islam who was not alive, the provisions of the law under which he had been convicted were not applicable. Following this judgment, there was an outbreak of violence, and, to pacify the protesters, the British government quickly enacted Section 295-A of the code. Although Patel was given police protection after his acquittal, he was stabbed to death while sitting in his bookshop. His assassin, Ilam Din, was convicted and executed, and 'acquired the position of a role model among many Muslims of the subcontinent. They are often urged by Muslim clerics to follow Illam Din Shaheed (the martyr) by killing those who offend the name of the Holy Prophet'.

In 1957, in *Ramji Lal Modi v The State of Uttar Pradesh*, the Supreme Court of India rejected a challenge to the constitutional validity of Section 295-A by the publisher of an article and cartoon which had caused offence to the Muslims of Uttar Pradesh. The publisher had been convicted and sentenced to 12 months' imprisonment and a fine. He argued unsuccessfully that Section 295-A was incompatible with his right to freedom of speech and expression guaranteed to him by Article 19 (1) (a) of the constitution because the offence of insulting the religion or religious beliefs of a class of citizens could be committed even where there was no likelihood of public disorder. The Supreme Court limited the scope of Section 295-A to 'the aggravated form of insult to religion where it is perpetrated with the deliberate and malicious intention of outraging the religious feelings'.

Article 19 of the constitution of India permits legislation to impose 'reasonable' restrictions on the fundamental right to freedom of expression. The word 'reasonable' can be interpreted as akin to the test of necessity or proportionality or as giving wider latitude to the legislative branch. In Ramji Lal Modi's case, the Supreme Court made Section 295-A compatible with human rights law only by requiring proof of the necessary mental element, but was not otherwise troubled by the vagueness and over-breadth of Section 295-A, and its chilling effect on freedom of speech; the court did not, however, interpret the meaning of 'reasonable' to accord with the principle of proportionality. Perhaps, in the absence of amending legislation, the Supreme Court's decision will be revisited in light of India's obligations under Article 19 of the UN International Covenant on Civil and Political Rights, and comparative jurisprudence elsewhere in the common law world.

Soli Sorabjee, the former Attorney General of India, observed almost 20 years ago that 'experience shows that criminal laws prohibiting hate speech and expression will encourage intolerance, divisiveness and unreasonable interference with freedom of expression. Fundamentalist Christians, religious Muslims and devout Hindus would then seek to invoke the criminal machinery against each other's religion, tenets or practices. That is what is increasingly happening in India today. We need not more repressive laws but more free speech to combat bigotry and to promote tolerance'.

Experience strongly supports Sorabjee's view. I will take as examples some tragic cases in India and Pakistan, but there are many others across and beyond the Commonwealth. They reveal laws and practices which are surely incompatible with international human rights standards. The misery and suffering they inflict is incalculable.

In India, in February 2009, Ravindra Kumar and Anand Sinha, the editor and publisher of the Calcutta-based *Statesman* daily newspaper, were arrested and charged under Section 295-A of the Penal Code with hurting the religious feelings of Muslims by republishing an article that first appeared in the UK newspaper the *Independent,* by Johann Hari, titled 'Why should I respect oppressive religions?' Sections of central Calcutta were paralysed by violent protests by a small group of Muslims who felt that the article slighted the Prophet Mohammed and insulted their religion.

Pakistan inherited the Indian Penal Code after partition. In the 1980s, General Muhammad Zia-ul-Haq's military dictatorship added draconian measures, including an offence punishable by death for using derogatory remarks in respect of the prophet, and another offence forbidding the Ahmadis, a Muslim group, from calling their places of worship mosques or performing any act which could outrage the feelings of Muslims. In 1986, a further offence was added prescribing death or life imprisonment for defiling the name of the prophet. The laws are frequently invoked to settle personal vendettas, or used by Islamist extremists as a cover to persecute religious minorities, and they are enforced not so much by the courts as by mob rule, murder and intimidation.

Pakistan has been an active supporter of the campaign by the Organisation of the Islamic Conference (OIC) to create global laws criminalising 'insults to religion'. On 25 March 2010, the UN Human Rights Council passed a resolution titled 'Combating Defamation of Religions' by a vote of 20 to 17. The resolution was proposed by Pakistan's permanent representative to the UN, Geneva, Zamir Akram, on behalf of the OIC. The resolution condemns what it calls a growing trend of 'negative stereotyping' of religions and religious figures. It also condemns the use of the media to target 'religious symbols' and 'venerated people'. Pakistan and the OIC are also at the forefront of an effort to amend the UN International Covenant for the Elimination of All Forms of Racial Discrimination to include a provision which would criminalise all 'insults to religion'.

Evils of religious intolerance

Yet to further criminalise 'insults' to religion will do nothing to alleviate an already tense climate of religious intolerance that exists in Pakistan. A report in 2009 by the Asian Human Rights Commission highlighted the case of Imran Masih, a Christian who was accused by his neighbour of burning a copy of the Quran. After several mosques announced his blasphemy over loudspeakers, his shop was set on fire, and he and his younger brother were beaten. He was taken into custody for blasphemy and in January 2010 he was sentenced by a Faisalabad court to life imprisonment.

In November 2010, a Punjabi court found Aasia Bibi guilty of insulting Islam and the Prophet Mohammed, in breach of Pakistan's blasphemy law, and sentenced her to death by hanging. According to reports, it all began with a quarrel over water. Aasia, an illiterate 45-year-old mother of five, offered water to some thirsty women who were working in the heat near a village in Pakistan's Punjab province, but was rebuffed. She was a Christian, they said, and so her water was unclean. She is alleged to have retaliated by insulting the prophet and Islam.

The local mullah took to his mosque's loudspeakers, exhorting his followers to take action against her. As a frenzied mob pursued her, the police intervened, taking her into custody. She was charged and convicted of insulting Islam and its prophet and, after 18 months in prison, became the first woman in Pakistan to be sentenced to death.

In December, the Imam of Peshawar's oldest mosque, Maulana Yousaf Qureshi, was reported to have offered a reward for anyone who killed her if the court failed to hang her. The call to violence was endorsed by *Nawa-i-Waqt*, Pakistan's second largest-selling newspaper. When the brave and liberal governor of Punjab, Salmaan Taseer, visited her in prison and urged her release, he was branded as an apostate by fundamentalist groups. In the fundamentalist view, apostasy, like blasphemy, is punishable by death. A report submitted to President Asif Ali Zardari, by the Minority Affairs Minister Shahbaz Bhatti, concluded that the blasphemy case against Aasia Bibi had been registered 'on grounds of personal enmity'. However, the High Court of Lahore blocked an offer by the president to pardon Aasia. And in January, the governor died for his beliefs, and his killer was praised by fanatics, including lawyers, who showered him with petals as he left court.

No one has been executed for blasphemy in Pakistan, and many blasphemy prosecutions are overturned by the appellate courts for lack of evidence; but, since 1990, at least ten Pakistanis accused of blasphemy have been killed while their cases were heard; and, in 1997, a Lahore judge who acquitted a teenager of blasphemy was gunned down.

Late last year, the former information minister of Pakistan, Sherry Rehman, introduced a bill in the National Assembly seeking to amend the Pakistan Penal Code and the Code of Civil Procedure to ensure that all citizens of Pakistan have an equal right to constitutional protection, and that miscarriages of justice in the name of blasphemy are avoided. The Jinnah Institute convened a roundtable meeting on 30 November 2010, where there was a consensus that the blasphemy laws should be amended to prevent the persecution of minorities. However, on 30 December, the government announced that it would not repeal the blasphemy law, and, days later, the interior minister, Rehman Malik, reportedly announced that he would personally shoot anyone found guilty of blasphemy.

Following the assassination of Taseer, Rehman received many death threats and told the BBC that Pakistan was now facing an existential threat from extremism. Shahbaz Bhatti, the only Christian in the cabinet, was threatened with beheading and refused to be intimidated from advocating the repeal of Pakistan's blasphemy laws. He was assassinated in March.

Asma Jahangir rightly argued, when she was UN Special Rapporteur on Freedom of Religion or Belief, that the concept of defamation of religions would, if sanctioned by international law, inevitably be used to undermine individual rights, since it would be used to legitimise anti-blasphemy laws which punish religious minorities, dissenters and non-believers. She has observed that 'if it was defamation to say that one religion was better than another, the result would be the religious persecution of those embarked on intellectual analysis of religions'.

That enlightened approach accords with the UN Human Rights Committee's recently published draft General Comment on Article 19 of the International Covenant on Civil and Political Rights 'on blasphemy prohibitions and other prohibitions of display of disrespect to a religion or other belief system'. The committee, many of whose members are from countries with large Muslim populations, has commented that such prohibitions 'may not discriminate in a manner that prefers one or certain religions or belief systems or their adherents over another, or religious believers over non-believers. Blasphemy laws should not be used to prevent or punish criticism of religious leaders or commentary on religious doctrine and tenets of faith. States parties should repeal criminal law provisions on blasphemy and regarding displays of disrespect for religion and other belief systems other than in the specific context of compliance with article 20 [of the covenant].'

In the United Kingdom, the leading English case on the common law crime of blasphemous libel was decided by the Law Lords in 1979, in the *Gay News* case. By a majority of three to two, and without the benefit of the constitutional framework of the Human Rights Act 1998 or full argument on the free speech issues, the Law Lords breathed new life into what had been regarded as an anachronistic and arbitrary relic of Tudor and Stuart times, when draconian powers of censorship had been exercised by the Ecclesiastical Courts and Court of Star Chamber, until they were taken over by the common law courts.

Blasphemy and the Church of England

The editor and publishers of *Gay News* were convicted on the grounds that they had 'unlawfully and wickedly published ... a blasphemous libel concerning the Christian religion namely an obscene poem and illustration vilifying Christ in His Life and in His crucifixion'. The editor was sentenced to nine months' imprisonment, suspended for 18 months, and fined £500, and the publishers were fined £1,000. The Court of Appeal dismissed their appeal, as did the House of Lords.

The poem, by James Kirkup, was entitled 'The Love that Dares to Speak its Name'. It was accompanied by a drawing illustrating its subject matter. It purported to describe in explicit detail homosexual acts with the body of Christ immediately after his death and to ascribe to him during his lifetime promiscuous homosexual practices with the apostles and other men. Each of the judges who decided the case expressed his profound disgust at the poem's offensive and obscene content.

The appellants' counsel in the *Gay News* case did not argue that blasphemous libel as a crime was unenforceable. With hindsight that is regrettable, because the Irish Supreme Court later decided that the same common law offence should not be recognised in Irish law because of its lack of legal certainty. Nor did counsel contend that the offence was incompatible with the convention and common law right to free speech.

Instead it was argued that blasphemy should not be regarded as an offence of strict liability, and that modern criminal jurisprudence required proof of a specific criminal intent to commit blasphemy. The only question in the appeal therefore was whether the mental element is satisfied by proof only of an intention to publish material which in the opinion of the jury is likely to shock and arouse resentment among believing Christians, or whether the prosecution must go further and prove that the accused, in publishing the material, in fact intended to produce that effect upon believers. Astonishingly, a majority of the Law Lords ruled that the offence was one of strict liability and that guilt does not depend on the accused having an intention to blaspheme.

However, in the wake of the *Gay News* case, the Law Commission for England and Wales undertook a review of the subject. After detailed study and consultation, in 1985 it recommended the abolition of the common law offences of blasphemy and blasphemous libel.

In 1991, in the case of *Choudhury*, a challenge was made to the publication of Salman Rushdie's novel, *The Satanic Verses*, seeking to prosecute

Mourners gather for the burial of Pakistani MP Shabhaz Bhatti, who was murdered after he supported reforms to the country›s blasphemy law. Credit: Mian Kursheed/Reuters

Rushdie and his publishers, Viking Penguin, for blasphemous libel and seditious libel. Reliance was placed upon Lord Scarman's judgment in the *Gay News* case, and upon the convention right to the enjoyment of religious freedom without discrimination, in an attempt to extend the common law offence of blasphemy to protect Islam against alleged insult. The case brought home the danger of retaining blasphemy as a criminal offence, because understandably it encouraged followers of other faiths to seek a non-discriminatory blasphemy law to protect their beliefs and practices against gross insult. One religion's faith is blasphemy to another religion; but to criminalise the defamation of all religions and beliefs (or secularist absences of religious belief) would also be divisive and severely restrictive of freedom of expression.

In April 2003, the House of Lords Select Committee on Religious Offences in England and Wales published its report on the reform of blasphemy laws. The Forum against Islamophobia and Racism, the Muslim Council of Britain and the Association of Muslim Lawyers gave evidence to the committee on what they saw as the need to extend the offence of blasphemy to all religions rather than to abolish it. The National Secular

Society argued for the abolition of the offence. It referred to the Indian Penal Code, recalling that, in January 1930, the Home Office had rejected a suggestion that the Indian Penal Code might be used as a blueprint for an extended blasphemy law.

The select committee noted that no blasphemy case has been prosecuted in England and Wales since the passage of the Human Rights Act 1998, but, 'it is a reasonable speculation that, as a consequence of that legislation any prosecution for blasphemy today – even one which met the known criteria – would be likely to fail or, if a conviction were secured, would probably be overturned on appeal'.

The select committee expressed its belief that 'there should be a degree of protection of faith, but there was no consensus among us about the precise form that it might take. We also agree that in any further legislation the protection should be equally available to all faiths, through both the civil and the criminal law.' However, at last, in 2008–9, the Westminster Parliament abolished all four common law offences of blasphemous, seditious, obscene and criminal libel.

One issue which was constantly raised during the long campaign for abolition of blasphemy as a crime was whether it should be replaced by legislation against incitement to religious hatred, similar to the prohibition of race hate speech. I agree with Soli Sorabjee that advocacy of objectionable doctrines, however strong and vigorous, but which lacks the ingredient of incitement to violence, cannot legitimately be prohibited and criminalised.

Tony Blair's Labour government did not heed this wise advice when, in a bid for votes during the 2005 general election, it promised to introduce a series of offences involving stirring up 'hatred against a group of people by reference to religious belief or lack of belief'. The proposed offences were political in two senses. First, they would punish or deter vigorous public criticism of the beliefs and practices of faith organisations and their supporters where that criticism was of a political nature. Secondly, the government's determination to create these offences was politically motivated – a targeted bid to woo British Muslim support.

The proposed legislation blurred the distinction between hate speech and blasphemy. Where hate speech involves incitement to imminent violence by those sympathetic to its hateful message, it may legitimately be criminalised. The concept of blasphemy involves a greater threat to freedom of expression because incitement to imminent violence is not an ingredient of the offence, and because the listener has wide discretion in deciding whether and when to take offence.

UN personnel carry the casket of one of the seven people killed in an attack on the organisation's operations in Mazar-e-Sharif, Afghanistan, 2 April 2011. The attack followed violent demonstrations against the burning of a Quran in Florida
Credit: Eric Kanalstein/AP/PA

In the event, New Labour was returned to power for a third term and the Racial and Religious Hatred Bill 2006 was introduced. The bill sought to give effect to the manifesto commitment to create new offences in the Public Order Act 1986 for stirring up religious hatred. The measure had the support of the Muslim Council of Britain but was strongly opposed by the opposition parties, most of the media, comedians and the evangelical Christian churches. It blurred the important distinctions between hate speech and blasphemy. But after considerable debate in the media and in both Houses of Parliament, and a rare government defeat in the House of Commons, it was radically changed by Lords amendments for which I was responsible. To protect freedom of expression, we confined the offences to 'threatening words or behaviour', and required a specific criminal intent, unlike the offences of stirring up racial hatred which apply to 'threatening, abusive or insulting words or behaviour', and if hatred is either intentional or 'likely' to be stirred up. And we also included the so-called 'English PEN clause' which provides that: 'Nothing in this Part shall be read or given effect in a way which prohibits or restricts discussion, criticism or expressions of antipathy, dislike, ridicule, insult or abuse of particular religions or the beliefs or practices of its adherents, or proselytising or urging adherents of a different religion or belief system to cease practising their religion or belief system.'

Religious hate speech, as well as homophobic hate speech, now has more latitude for free expression than does race hate speech, under British criminal law protecting public order. There is no political appetite to bring the race hate offences into line with the other speech hate crimes.

Asma Jahangir noted in her 2008 report about her mission to the UK that almost all of those she met agreed that there is a very satisfactory amount of freedom of religion and belief in the UK, and that many of them stated that 'the situation of their respective communities was far better than those countries where they had emigrated from'. Their countries of origin, in the Indian sub-continent and elsewhere, have stringent criminal laws against blasphemy and defamation of religion, as well as the many public order offences. They do not seem to have enhanced freedom of religion or promoted mutual tolerance and respect. Nor have the vague and sweepingly broad offences against religion in the Penal Codes achieved their historic aims. Violence by fundamentalist fanatics and the tyranny of the mob are all too prevalent.

The time is ripe across the common law world to consider whether this legacy from the British Empire should be replaced by modern, carefully tailored laws designed to promote both freedom of expression and freedom of religion while giving necessary protection against public disorder and the incitement of violence and discrimination. ❐

40(2): 147/164
DOI: 10.1177/0306422011409291
www.indexoncensorship.org

Lord Lester of Herne Hill QC practises constitutional and human rights law at Blackstone Chambers and has argued many leading cases in the two European courts, and British and Commonwealth courts. He is a Liberal Democrat peer and has introduced a number of influential bills, most recently on defamation reform. This is an edited and updated version of his keynote address to the 17th Commonwealth Lawyers Association Conference in Hyderabad, India, on 8 February 2011

THE CLOAK

In the first chapter of his new novel, celebrated writer **Ibrahim al Koni** draws on the rich heritage of Arabic political allegory to explore totalitarianism

Ibrahim al Koni (b 1948) is Libya's leading literary figure. A Tuareg from the south of the country, al Koni writes in a distinctly allegorical and classical Arabic style that draws heavily on the myths and folk traditions of the Sahara. The author of more than 70 titles – including novels, collections of short stories and aphorisms, and historical studies – al Koni has lived outside Libya for decades, first as a student at the Maxim Gorky Institute of Literature in Moscow, then as a journalist and diplomat in eastern Europe. For the past two decades, he has made Switzerland his home. His novels have won prizes across the world and his works have been translated into many languages.

'The Cloak' is the first chapter of al Koni's 2008 novel Al Waram (The Tumour). *The work is a thinly-veiled allegory of the madness and tragedy of Muammar Gaddafi's rule. The central character of the novel, Asanay, refuses to relinquish the cloak of power that has been given to him by the chief – with bloody and disturbing results for all. Few novels have predicted the future as vividly as* The Tumour. *With his typical philosophical style, al Koni strips back the authoritarianism of his native land to show the fable and legend beneath.* Elliott Colla

Asanay awoke to find the leather cloak clinging to his body. He had fallen asleep on the mat while still wearing it. He was fastidious about removing the magnificent garment when sleep approached. He would fold it carefully before putting it away in its own sack. He would wipe off the specks of dust with a gentle brush of his hand. He would blow off the dirt with his mouth, or even lick it off with his tongue. He never stored it away without wrapping it first in a piece of woven silk. Never before today had his strength betrayed him like this. Never before had sleep conquered him while he still wore the cloak. Was it perspiration – relentless, sticky sweat – that poured out of his body when he surrendered to sleep? If sweat was the symptom, then water would be the antidote.

But could he use water to pry his body free without also ruining the splendid robe? Asanay shouted at his servants, raining insults on the bastard that desert tribes call 'sleep'.

A large man with thick features appeared in the doorway. The man bowed his naked head of black-and-white hair. 'Master,' he murmured.

Asanay wasted no time to lay into the man, 'How many times do I have to tell you? There is no master but our chief! If not for his generosity and beneficence, we would not even be here.'

The man's voice faded to a mumble, 'I beg your pardon, my…' He caught himself before whispering the word. Asanay shouted, 'Bring me some water! Just look at what this nasty sweat has done to our master's robe!'

The slave made to leave, but Asanay stopped him, 'Wait! Do you think you can take it off without using water? Let's try.'

The man wheeled back. He grabbed the thick, furry collar and began to yank on it. He went on pulling until Asanay began to scream in pain, 'What are you doing, you wretch?! Are you trying to rip out my shoulder?'

The large man bent over until he was nearly laying across his master's shoulders. Asanay yelled again, 'Get away, you disgusting creature! Are you trying to suffocate me with your stench?'

The slave took a step back. His eyes spun around in their sockets like a chameleon's. He whispered, 'I'm afraid I can't do it, my lord!'

Asanay shot him a look of surprise, 'What are you saying, you dog?'

The man let out a loud breath, then stood erect. 'The robe has melted into your skin, my lord,' he muttered.

Asanay looked carefully at his arms. The leather patches had grafted themselves all the way to his wrist. The leather strips, braided with gold thread, had folded themselves into the flesh. Only the skin of his palms and fingers remained bare. With trembling fingers, he felt at his chest and discovered that there also the robe hugged at him. He tugged at the long leather tassels that dangled from the collar and tore a cry of pain from his throat. The tassels, like the magnificent robe, had fused into the meat of his body. He called for witch doctors. There was no other choice if one hoped to escape such a wicked trap.

The witch doctor arrived. Wrapped from head to toe in black, his tall frame was grave and sombre. The man's skin was copper itself and his eyes like empty sockets.

Asanay put himself in the man's hands. The witch doctor circled around him again and again. He fondled and felt at the patched folds of living leather. He pulled at the fur collar around Asanay's throat. With long slender fingers, he traced the seams of the robe across Asanay's entire body. Then, at last, he exhaled with a loud breath and sat down cross-legged in front of the afflicted man. Even before the other man began to speak, Asanay could read the ruin in his eyes.

'I must confess,' the witch doctor finally sighed. 'It's a peculiar kind of magic.'

Asanay stared at his face for minutes, wrestling with his sense of desperation. 'How does this confession concern me?'

The man's vacant stare didn't budge. His body never moved. In an absent tone, he merely commented, 'All I meant to say was that I've never seen such magic in the oases before.'

Asanay fell silent. From time to time, he stole glances at his companion while fiddling with the leather scraps of his skin. He finally opened his mouth, 'Did someone do this to me?' The emptiness in the witch doctor's eyes fell away to reveal a haze behind them. 'I can say with confidence that this was done to you deliberately. But what I cannot tell you is whether the hand behind this was human.'

Asanay studied the witch doctor for minutes. At last, he smiled. 'What do you mean?'

The witch doctor did not hesitate. 'There are many different kinds of schemes and spells. Those hatched by men are the least of them.'

Curiosity twinkled in Asanay's eye. 'What are you saying?'

This time the witch doctor took his time before answering. 'The schemes of the creator are a thousand times worse than those of his creations.'

Asanay fell silent. Aloud, the witch doctor asked, 'Have you ever done something to anger the jinn?'

Puzzled, Asanay studied the man. Then he lowered his head and answered, 'I don't remember doing anything to them on purpose. But when the fates make a man a leader of the people, he will eventually make a mistake. He will inevitably cross the jinn, whether he does so deliberately or not.'

Tiled wall outside a mosque in Tripoli, Libya
Credit: Liquid Light/Alamy

The witch doctor muttered, 'True. But you should try to remember something specific.'

Asanay looked for compassion from the man, like someone awaiting punishment. 'I committed no sin.'

But the witch doctor was unrelenting. 'All of us sin. Not just once, but time and again. We sin every time we take a step.'

Asanay smiled painfully without raising his eyes from the mat. 'I told you that I don't remember committing any sin against the heavens. As God is my witness – I've done no wrong. Unless you call pleasing women in bed a sin.' He laughed, 'Am I being punished for that?'

The witch doctor didn't laugh at the joke. The sockets of his eyes filled again with emptiness. 'Don't talk about your sleeping with women. Tell me about love. Have you been in love?'

A laugh escaped from Asanay's lips. 'According to desert customs, what's the difference? Aren't they the same thing?'

The witch doctor's reply was icy. 'Not at all. To sleep with women is not to love. Not by our customs, at least.'

Asanay looked at him in disbelief. 'Ah, yes. Now I remember. Your type calls this sort of thing "appetite".'

'Very good. Now, have you ever been in love?'

Asanay's nervous silence dragged on until a nasty whisper came out of his mouth, 'Never. No, that's not right. I have love. I have loved the chief's cloak more than anything else in the world.' He snickered, then began to laugh so hard that the servants came running from around the house. With a flick of his hand, he told them to go away. As Asanay's fingers wiped the tears from his eyes, the other man began to speak with the voice of an oracle who could only pronounce the truth. 'Whoever truly loves a thing becomes part of it.'

Asanay raised his head. Daunted, he looked at the man sitting across from him. The witch doctor repeated the phrase again, then corrected himself. 'I mean, he who loves a thing more than he should becomes part of that thing.'

Asanay stared at the man for minutes. He began to notice how emaciated the old copper-brown man was. Bones protruded from every joint in his body. Then he finally glimpsed the milky whiteness of the man's eyes. They were the eyes of a man whose companions think he can see, but never realise he only ever looks out onto the void.

Asanay said, 'I don't want my enemies to take pleasure in my trouble.'

The witch doctor's empty eyes fixed on him as he mumbled, 'If you don't want to give your enemies reason to rejoice, you must make a sacrifice. You must give up something valuable. The most valuable thing you can offer.'

Afraid to hear what that would be, Asanay asked, 'Offer up something valuable?'

A slight smile glimmered on the lips of the witch doctor. He cleared his throat. 'My lord, we will never be free as long as we have neglected to give up those things we hold most dear. Those things we love more than we ought to.'

Asanay muttered, 'What do you mean?'

The witch doctor answered with a question, 'Why not take off the cloak?'

'Take it off?'

When the witch doctor spoke again, all human warmth had quit his voice. 'It is far easier for us to willingly give up a possession than to have it snatched away by force.'

A look of disdain sketched itself on Asanay's lips. 'Am I listening to a witch doctor, or a soothsayer?'

'When it suits him, a witch doctor may borrow a soothsayer's tongue. And vice versa, my lord. Don't they say that we are both moulded from the same desert soil?'

'And don't they also say that it is never right to trade one's tongue for another?'

The witch doctor sat quietly for minutes. When he spoke, his question shocked his companion. 'Does my lord love the cloak too much?' Asanay repressed a wicked laugh and thought he might as well answer questions with questions. 'Is there a creature in this great desert who does not love this cloak with all his heart?'

The witch doctor smiled enigmatically before responding, 'The danger is not that we might love a gift. It is that we might love the gift more than the giver.'

'What do you mean?'

'Our downfall resides not in loving the cloak you wear. But in loving it more than the person to whom it belongs – the person who gave it to you.'

Worry spread across Asanay's face. He now began to speak like someone defending himself before a crowd of accusers. 'We express our gratitude to the giver by loving his gift.'

'Gratitude for a gift is one thing, my lord, but love is something else.'

'How do wise men expect us to love someone while holding back our appreciation for his beneficence?'

A look of severity flashed across the witch doctor's face, and the bones of his brow began to protrude a little more. 'We express our love for the giver by our indifference toward the gift.' His voice was defiant.

'Bullshit!' Asanay laughed. He choked back more laughter and murmured, 'Are you telling me I should give away my cloak to one of the local oasis layabouts? Is that really the best way for me to thank the chief for his gift?'

The witch doctor stubbornly continued. 'The only way to express our love is to relinquish the dearest thing we hold in our hand.'

Asanay looked at the man with fury in his eyes. 'Do you love the chief?'

'Of course.'

'Would you offer him your son as token of your love?'

For a moment, the witch doctor said nothing. He closed eyes already hidden behind pale clouds. 'Children are not things that can be held in the hand. We do not have the right to sacrifice them as tokens of love.'

Asanay exhaled with relief. Intoxicated by the victory he sensed was near, he asked, 'Really?'

The witch doctor stopped him with a wave of his hand. 'In spite of this, I would not hold back anything, not even children, if I was sure that the chief required such a sacrifice.'

'What? Are you saying the chief requires a sacrifice?'

The witch doctor hesitated for a moment. 'I only said that I would not hold anything back if I were certain ...'

'What does that mean?'

'Only what I said, my lord. Children are the one kind of creature in this desert that should never be sacrificed. It is we who should sacrifice ourselves for their sake. Only if we were certain that the chief required it would we be justified in making such a horrible sacrifice.'

Asanay held his tongue. He thought it over for a while before he finally spoke. 'I never thought that the chief needed my love. If I were certain ...'

His voice disappeared. The witch doctor sighed. 'I'm not talking about an exchange of this for that. We are obliged to love the chief, not because he loves us, but because it's our duty to love him.'

Asanay mumbled absently, 'I may not have always known how to show my gratitude, but I've never once been ungrateful toward him.'

'To be grateful is to show respect in exchange for a gift. It's never the same as love.'

A silence fell over the two men. Then Asanay shouted, like he'd just made a precious discovery, 'Very well. Do you want the truth? The truth is I was never once certain whether the chief's cloak was a sign of love at all.'

The witch doctor held his tongue. He bowed forward until his veil touched the mat. 'The cloak is merely a jacket. An empty piece of clothing to put on and take off. It is not the giver of the clothing who fills it, but the one to whom it has been given.'

Asanay leaned forward and whispered, 'Explain.'

'The jacket is nothing but a garment made of leather. It is neither good nor bad. Whatever power it has comes solely from wearing it. And what matters is how you wear it.'

Asanay turned his face away. 'I have only used its power to do what had to be done.'

The witch doctor looked sceptically at his companion. 'That's what you say.'

Asanay glared at him and shouted, 'Explain yourself!'

The witch doctor hesitated for a moment. He kept his head bowed low as he spoke.'I cannot do so, my lord, until you grant me permission to speak freely and without fear of reprisal.'

Asanay looked curiously at the man. 'Since when do witch doctors in the desert go asking for permission to speak?'

'My lord, do not forget that we are not in the desert.'

'Isn't this oasis an integral part of the great desert?'

'Not at all, my lord. Not at all. Ever since this oasis was surrounded by a wall, it became something by itself. It used to be part of the desert, but now it's become detached.'

Asanay's voice was puffed up when he spoke, 'Walls? Since when were squat piles of mud brick the same as mountain ranges of stone?'

'Just because the walls are made of mud does not mean they fail to perform their function.'

Enraged, Asanay rose. 'Are you insinuating it was wrong to build it?'

The witch doctor held his tongue for a minute before daring to answer. 'Of course. It is always a mistake to create obstacles and barriers.'

'My God. Are you being serious?'

'Were it not for this sin, the cloak would not have led my Lord astray, nor would it have become the topic that sits on every tongue.'

Asanay grumbled in his seat. He looked at his companion as if he now saw him for the first time. 'What are you referring to?'

The witch doctor's eyes were emptier than ever. 'I thought you'd given me permission to speak freely.'

A silence fell over them again. Asanay finally spoke. 'Of course. I gave you freedom to speak, but not so you would fill my ears with the slander that sits on the tongues of my enemies.'

Um el Ma oasis and sand dunes, Libya
Credit: Konrad Wothe/ LOOK Die Bildagentur der Fotografen GmbH/Alamy

The witch doctor curled himself up tight. Not knowing what to do with his hands, he began to rub them together. He let out a moan, then spoke. 'The truth is I don't know where to begin.'

Asanay said nothing – perhaps so as to rise above the level of chitchat, perhaps to snatch some insight from the mouth of a wise man.

The witch doctor finally spoke. 'I do not need to remind you, my lord, about the wicked qualities of the robe, for its story is known by every tongue in the desert. It was for this reason that our ancestors shunned it and abstained from using it. The most powerful weapon they had against its effect was to show it indifference.'

Asanay clung to his silence. The witch doctor went on. 'Those who shunned it likened it to a special kind of passion which, if sated, would consume you and if held in restraint, would protect you. So, my lord, which of these things have you done with your treasure?'

Asanay stared at the witch doctor with a terrifying sort of curiosity. The man had suddenly turned into a beast of fables and legends before Asanay's eyes. The witch doctor finally spoke again. 'You should have taken the jacket and put it to good use. Instead, the jacket took possession of you and used you in the worst possible way.'

Asanay began to get up, his face trembling. The witch doctor noticed the malice in his eyes and blurted out, 'Have I overstepped your indulgence?'

Asanay roared, 'I did not give you permission to speak because I wanted to listen to you pour the whispers and lies of enemies into my ears. Watch yourself.'

Asanay now leapt to his feet, his body shaking with rage. The witch doctor stood as well. The two men stood facing one another in silence. The witch doctor made to leave, but the robe's owner caught him before he could get away. 'You are deluded to think I would give up what I hold in my hand.'

Asanay tugged fitfully at the hem of the cloak to conceal his anger – but the pain was too much. He turned pale and began to moan uncontrollably. ❐

Translated by Elliott Colla

40(2): 166/176
DOI: 10.1177/0306422011409492
www.indexoncensorship.org